LIKE SHOOTING RAPIDS
IN THE DARK

Where there is no vision, the people perish.

PROVERBS 29:18

*"If a nation expects to be ignorant and free
. . . it expects what never was and never will be."*

THOMAS JEFFERSON
(LETTER TO COL. CHARLES YANCEY,
JANUARY 6, 1816)

LIKE SHOOTING RAPIDS IN THE DARK

Selected Writings on Education by

BILLY O. WIREMAN

EDITED BY DICK GOODE AND BOB WHALEN

NEWSOUTH BOOKS

MONTGOMERY

NewSouth Books
P.O. Box 1588
Montgomery, AL 36102

Library of Congress Cataloging-in-Publication Data

ISBN 1-58838-088-2

Design by Randall Williams
Printed in the United States of America

CONTENTS

FOREWORD

There is no issue more central to the American experiment today than education. And few people know more about education than Billy O. Wireman. Billy Wireman, the former president of Queens College, in Charlotte, North Carolina, and before that, the president of Eckerd College in St. Petersburg, Florida, had thirty-three years of hands-on experience in managing a private college. He raised millions and millions of dollars; balanced budgets; wooed donors; inspired faculty; moved the recalcitrant and removed the incompetent. He created, directed, and managed thousands of projects both large and small.

Yet Wireman was and is far more than a skilled manager. He is an educational visionary with an intense sense of where American education needs to go and a keen sense of how to get there. Modest, self-deprecating, self-critical, President Billy Wireman has been aflame with a passion for students, teachers, and education. Not everyone will embrace all his ideas, but we would all be poorer without them.

As surely as the sun will rise, America's democratic experiment will fail if we lose sight of what education can and must do. Anyone seriously interested in education—and that should be every American—will profit from Billy Wireman's insights, arguments, and visions.

Rolfe Neill is the former editor of the Charlotte Observer.

Introduction

BY DICK GOODE AND BOB WHALEN

T his is a true story: Several years ago, a terrifying volcanic eruption devastated much of the world north of Manila in the Philippines. A number of churches in Charlotte, North Carolina (like churches around the world) hurriedly collected emergency supplies and shipped them off. A delegation from the Charlotte churches went with the supplies. They landed in Manila, helped load the supplies onto trucks, and then set off up into the Filipino outback, off to a little village about as far from anything in the world as it could be. When they arrived in the village, the mayor and the village leaders hosted the group from Charlotte at a little ceremony. The mayor, speaking in Tagalog, thanked the Charlotteans for coming and for helping in this time of grievous need. A representative of the Filipino government translated.

"Where in the U.S. are you Americans from?" the mayor asked.

"Well," the Americans replied, "we're sure you've never heard of it, but we're from the state of North Carolina."

"Oh, yes," the mayor said, brightening, "where in North Carolina?"

"Well," the Americans replied, "we're sure you've never heard of it, but we're from a city called Charlotte." The translator translated.

"Oh, Charlotte!" the mayor exclaimed. "Do you know Billy Wireman?"

Of course the Charlotteans knew Billy O. Wireman. In fact, around the world, it seems hard to find someone who doesn't. If you're one of those rare souls, you're in for a treat. Let us introduce Dr. Billy O. Wireman to you.

In 1968, at the age of 35, Billy O. Wireman was the youngest college president in the United States. Named to lead the newly created Florida Presbyterian College, in St. Petersburg, Dr. Wireman helped transform that struggling newborn into a prosperous and respected liberal arts college, now known as Eckerd College.

Then in 1978, the trustees of Queens College, in Charlotte, North Carolina, called on Dr. Wireman to come to Queens's rescue. Founded in 1857, descended from Scots-Irish Presbyterian schools that pre-dated the American Revolution, Queens College was in big trouble in 1978. A woman's college, it had tumbled into a potentially fatal downward spiral. Enrollment was way off, revenues were way down, debts were piling up. An attempt to right the college by massive cuts and layoffs only made the school even less attractive and all but destroyed morale. The trustees considered closing Queens, or merging it with another institution, but the optimists among the trustees, like then-chairman Joe Grier, prevailed on their colleagues to give the young academic miracle-worker from St. Petersburg a chance.

The optimists were proved right. In his long tenure at Queens College, Billy Wireman proved himself to be a turn-around artist, not to mention a high-wire walker and more than once a magician. It was hard-going, to be sure, much harder than even the pessimists among the trustees had feared, but Queens righted itself, stabilized, underwent repairs while setting full sail, and transformed itself into a smart, prosperous, energetic little liberal arts college. During his time at Queens's helm, Dr. Wireman increased the college's endowment more than tenfold; he created its evening programs, expanded its graduate programs, and set up its business school; he inspired a sweeping redesign of the college's undergraduate curriculum, which now includes a solid foundation in the liberal arts (the college's "Core Program"), an internship program which is integrated into the undergraduate curriculum, and an international experience program which involves an astonishing 90 percent of Queens students (nationally, fewer than 10 percent of American undergraduates have any serious international experience). Dr. Wireman would be the last to take credit for this transformation, and the first to point out the college's on-going challenges, but there simply is no denying the transformation Billy Wireman brought to Queens. During Queens's ten-year reaccreditation review by the Southern Association of Colleges and Schools in 2001, two of the college's major components were commended: its mission of educating students for "Noble Lives, Productive Careers, and Global Citizenship," and its year-long internship program (cited as "a model for the country").

When Dr. Wireman announced a year ago that he would retire this year, the *Charlotte Observer* made this observation in a July 30, 2001, editorial:

> Billy Wireman's retirement as president of Queens College will mark the end of one of the most amazing turnabouts in higher education. . . . The once sickly school has become a beehive of intellectual activity. . . . Money is important, but Dr. Wireman never forgot that the measure of a school is not its balance sheet, but its success in teaching and learning. An avid reader, writer, traveler, and teacher, he might well be the model for the school he leads: insatiably curious, pragmatic, yet adventuresome, eager to meet new challenges but rooted in enduring values.

We were there for much of the "turnabout" that the *Observer* mentioned as having been wrought during Wireman's tenure. We saw it with our own eyes. And so did much of the academic world.

Queens is hardly famous. But when serious people talk seriously about education, about higher education, about the future of the liberal arts and especially those colleges dedicated to the liberal arts, Billy Wireman and Queens come up sooner rather than later. On the eve of his retirement, Dr. Wireman is now one of the longest-serving college presidents in American history. It seems that he knows everyone in higher education; three of Dr. Wireman's vice presidents have gone on to be college presidents and many other colleagues have gone off to serve in a host of other institutions. As a fundraiser, consultant, and educational advisor, Dr. Wireman has traveled around the country and around the world; no doubt he has enough frequent-flyer miles to take him to Neptune and back. And in his current home town of Charlotte, North Carolina, Billy O. Wireman has become an institution. A committed Christian, he is a leader in his local church; he has worked with innumerable civic organizations; and he has chaired both the Charlotte World Affairs Council and the Community Relations Commission.

They say that everyone in the world is connected, that my friend has a friend who has a cousin who has a sister-in-law whose niece went to school with you. If it's true that only six degrees of separation stand between us all, then Billy Wireman has transcended at least five of them and is hard at work on the sixth. Sooner or later, everyone knows Billy Wireman and he knows them.

He was born in Quicksand, Kentucky, and raised outside of Louisville. He studied at Georgetown College of Kentucky, and after a stint in the Marine Corps in the 1950s, he went on to graduate study at the University of Kentucky. Billy Wireman loved sports: his field was physical education, and his dream was to be a physical education teacher and coach. At Kentucky he came very close to that dream. For a year he was an assistant to one of the gods of basketball, Adolf Rupp (and if you have the time, he would love to tell you some Rupp stories). In 1960, after earning his degree, Billy Wireman joined the faculty of the newly opened Florida Presbyterian College, in St. Petersburg, Florida.

Florida Presbyterian soon learned that it had much more than a young physical education instructor on its staff. Billy Wireman proved to have a knack at organizing, a boundless energy for creating and pursuing projects, an insatiable curiosity about just about everything, and a passion for education (he earned a doctorate in education from Vanderbilt University's Peabody School of Education before joining the faculty). Florida Presbyterian's leaders asked their young physical education professor to serve as Dean of Men, then as vice president for development, then they surprised everyone, including Billy Wireman, by asking him to assume the college's presidency.

Dr. Wireman served as Florida Presbyterian's president for nine years, in the process transforming the school into Eckerd College and earning a name for himself as an innovative college-builder. Going to Queens College in 1978 was a gamble, but it reflected both his love of a hurdle as well as his unflinching commitment to the model of education incarnated in the small liberal arts college. In an age of mega-universities, Billy Wireman was not only convinced that the liberal arts college still had an honored and vital place, but he was determined to revive and reinvigorate the small college alternative—an education rooted in small classes, vigorous teaching, rigorous programs, and an unswerving dedication to the promise of liberal arts.

When Dr. Wireman left Eckerd College, it was ranked as one of America's top liberal arts colleges. The highly respected academic journal, *Change Magazine*, in December 1977, had this to say about his tenure at Eckerd in an article entitled "The Vision of Billy Wireman":

> The history of innovative higher education has produced its share of charismatic leaders . . . who have managed to convey to their faculty and students a sense of their own importance and their university's place in the sun. If the leader has been particularly daring and imaginative, leader and college become synonymous in people's minds. Such is the case with Billy Wireman and

Eckerd College. "In a real sense, Eckerd College was Billy Wireman, and vice versa. It came down to that," was the way one faculty member put it.

Billy Wireman has gladly given his life to the liberal arts. The term "liberal arts" is, of course, a kind of poetic "conceit," a dynamic metaphor. "Arts" refer to the abilities one needs not only to survive but to prosper in one's world. In ancient Greece and Rome those abilities included, above all, skill at rhetoric and dialectic, the cut and thrust of argument in the public forum. In modern America, rhetoric and dialectic remain important but today some understanding of science, technology, and economics, all in a global perspective, is unquestionably important. Education must be about helping people construct productive careers and helping communities build a more prosperous world.

But education must include, too, a "liberal," that is, "liberating," dimension. Education must "enlighten"; it must free one from the here and now, from the way things are and the powers that be; it must fire the imagination and thrill the soul. How? By plunging students into the strange worlds of the past, or the future, or into the worlds on the other side of the oceans. By encouraging questions, and debate, and controversy; by refusing to accept the "as is" as all there is.

The liberal arts, for Billy Wireman, are central to an

education for "citizenship." Citizenship means active participation in a world of equals, in which each person is respected, consulted, and above all free to grow. It is a world in which we are all accountable to ourselves and to each other. Citizenship occurs not in an "arena" where the carnivorous can satisfy their appetites, nor even in a "family" in which the philanthropic care for the incompetent, but in a republic in which free and equal citizens work together to forge the future. This citizenship must be, in the twenty-first century, a global citizenship, and the ideal must be a cosmopolitan, inclusive republic in which "others" become "neighbors."

Such a republic, moreover, should be explicitly dedicated to certain transcendent values. A "value-free" education would be, from Billy Wireman's perspective, monstrous. It is essential to distinguish between truth and lies, between love and hate, between the profound and the superficial and to honor the better and disdain the worse. This is not to advocate ideology or dogmatism but to do the very opposite, for the values integral to a liberal arts education—free speech and free thought, tolerance, critical thinking, objectivity and honesty—are the precise opposites of ideology and dogmatism.

Billy O. Wireman has been inspired, and has inspired others, with a compelling vision of what American education could be at its very best. He has forged and refined this vision over the years, in countless articles and speeches.

On the eve of his retirement, scores of friends have asked him to sort his ideas into a single volume, to hone his wisdom into words that could become an inheritance for another generation of students and teachers.

He was reluctant to do so, partly because he still had a college to run, partly because he had a retirement to plan (which, knowing Billy Wireman, almost certainly will be anything but retiring), partly because he was hard at work on a book about his own teachers (*Lessons from the Big Guys*, he likes to call it) and partly because of his deeply ingrained modesty. Reluctant to cast himself as an "expert," let alone "visionary" (for heaven's sake!), Dr. Wireman demurred. Would he mind, then, if someone else looked through his writings and edited them into some sort of order? Of course not, he replied.

We quickly volunteered to do just that. We volunteered not only because of our deep affection for Billy Wireman but also because of our conviction that what he has said and thought over the years is rich and smart and deserves not just to be preserved but to be broadcast. As we read through thirty years of his writings, we were often astonished at his prescience and his wisdom.

So the words that follow are mostly Billy Wireman's. We've done the editing and have added some explanatory notes. There is a serious, earnest, Presbyterian side to Dr. Wireman, and that side predominates in much of what follows. This is, after all, serious thinking about a serious topic. But we hope that what also comes through is his electric zest for life and love of learning.

"Guys, this will be an adventure!" Dr. Wireman likes to say on the eve of yet another daring project. Education is an adventure or it is nothing. This little book, then, is much more than a recollection of the past; it is a beckoning to the future.

John Locke wrote in *Some Thoughts Concerning Education:*

> I think I may say, that of all the Men we meet with, nine parts of ten are what they are, Good or Evil, useful or not, by their Education. 'Tis that which makes the great Difference in Mankind: The little and almost insensible Impressions on our tender Infancies, have very important and lasting Consequences. And there 'tis as in the Fountains of some Rivers, where a gentle Application of the Hand turns the flexible Waters into Channels, that make them take quite contrary Courses, and by this little Direction given them first in the Source, they receive different Tendencies, and arrive, at last, at very remote and distant Places.

We agree with Locke. However powerful and intractable human nature, we think that some great percent of who men and women are is a result of their education; that this education, though begun in "infancy," continues on for many years; and that this education, more than any-thing else, is responsible for the places people go and the things they do and see. To be a teacher is a vital and ennobling vocation. Billy Wireman is not only a great college president, but a great teacher, too (Lord knows, he has carried us to "remote and distant places"!). He has important lessons to teach us all.

We struggled to find the best way to organize Dr. Wireman's selected writings on education. We originally planned to sort them into tidy categories, but realized as we read through the material, that they should be left as they grew, organically, progressively, shaped importantly by their historical ecology, and above all, alive. We do not wish to be intellectual taxidermists. Instead, we want to be magicians, conjuring up something of the energy, vitality, and enthusiasm, and yes, magic, of Dr. Wireman's ideas about education.

No, this is not a book for everyone. But it is a book for anyone seriously interested in what every citizen should be interested in: education and the construction of the future. We have, with Dr. Wireman's permission, edited for clarity, but the words are his own. They are worth listening to.

What? You're one of the rare souls who doesn't know Billy O. Wireman? Read on. You're in for a treat.

Like Shooting Rapids
in the Dark

[Thinking about anything always begins somewhere. The richest thought evolves organically from one's own life and loves. This is a book about education, but not as some disembodied abstraction. It is a book about education as one person tried to think about it, live within it, and put it into practice. Billy O. Wireman is that person. For more than forty years, Wireman lived education. What follows, more or less in the order in which he wrote them, are his thoughts about what education was, is, and could be.]

Why Not Join the College Community?

[As a young man, Wireman loved sports. His great ambition was to be a physical education teacher and a coach. He joined Florida Presbyterian College in the early 1960s as a physical education instructor. Even then, Wireman wasn't content to think solely within the world of sports. From his apprentice days as a teacher, he fretted about education. Here, in one of his very first published writings, he worries about the tendency of coaches and athletes to segregate themselves in the gym and on the playing field. He pleads with physical education instructors, coaches, and athletes to "join the college community."]

A criticism made of physical educators is that they are not well-rounded and tend to isolate themselves in their own discipline. As physical educators, there are several things we can do to be more effective members of the college community.

• BE WELL INFORMED ABOUT EDUCATION. We should attempt to broaden our knowledge and become more interested in problems of education not directly related to physical education. We may not be able to solve these problems, but we should realize that one of the purposes of education is to develop in people a discriminatory power which enables them to read about, discuss, and ponder over issues; on the basis of rational, objective judgment to differentiate fact from opinion, political ambition from genuine concern; and then to use these discernments to arrive at some considered and intelligent impressions concerning these issues. What are the characteristics of an educated person? Education's problems are our problems.

• BE AWARE OF SHARING. We should also be more sensitive to the many common denominators of physical education and other subjects. With the historian we share a wealth of common interests; physical education, at various times in history, has been appropriated for political purposes. It has not been uncommon for people's religious beliefs to influence their feelings about physical activity; consequently physical education and religion are inextricably mixed. With the natural sciences we also find common bonds.

• SUPPORT OTHER COLLEGE ACTIVITIES. We feel that our activities are important and should be supported by the other members of the community. By the same token, we should feel a responsibility to reciprocate with a loyalty to the other college functions.

• BE AN ARTICULATE SPOKESMAN. The physical educator should strive to be a scholar in the field. The physical educator should have the discipline in proper perspective and remember that the primary aim of an institution is scholarship, a scholarship that results in growth and maturity in students on a wide and diversified front and not in the accumulation of abstract and unrelated facts. I cannot support the thesis that physical education is doomed to an inferior place in the college curriculum and in the minds of discerning educators. We must assert time and again the importance of physical education.

• RESPECT IS EARNED, IT IS NOT AUTOMATIC. Physical education must demand from its own practitioners the necessary standards of excellence to make improvements. These demands must be initiated internally and with an unrelenting desire for excellence.

("WHY NOT JOIN THE COLLEGE COMMUNITY?" *Florida J.O.H.P.E.R.,* JANUARY 1961.)

Educate for Freedom

[The issues of physical education, though, can't be seen in isolation from wider issues in education. Still a young P.E. instructor in 1962, Billy Wireman argues that physical education has to be seen in a much wider perspective.]

In discussing possible future directions in physical education we must first ask ourselves *what type of citizen* the coming years will demand. My answer is that the coming years will demand a sensitive, disciplined, enlightened, concerned, "universe-oriented," productive, "physically educated" citizen, who has the ability and desire to preserve and extend freedom, in short, we must either begin to educate for freedom or abandon the idea.

It is imperative now as never before that the physical educator take an integrated approach to the teaching and learning process. To be an educator means to have some ideas as to when one is being educated, what education is and is not, how people learn, what should be taught, and why. These are turbulent times; the circumstances of our times have created anew the need for a more varied and broad background within the scope of each academic discipline—a deep, comprehensive experience. To teach only within the narrow confines of one field today is to fail to share with the one being taught the full meaning of what one teaches. We must, then, not only be concerned with and sensitive to what has gone before but also what the current status of our profession is. Then on the basis of "what has been" and what "is" we must decide "what ought to be." The only way our theories can be well-grounded and sound is to have some understanding of what has gone before. Hippocrates addresses himself to the importance of having our theories well-grounded in the following passage: "One must pay attention not to plausible theorizing, but to experience and reason together. I agree that theorizing is to be approved, provided that it is based on facts, and systematically makes its deductions from what is observed. But conclusions drawn from unaided reason can hardly be serviceable; only those drawn from observed fact."

We are active participants in the most challenging and dangerous era in history. We physical educators must continually define and develop a "cutting edge" to our roles; rather than hold on and conserve we must push forward and create, constantly seeking new horizons.

Becoming what you are physically is a vital part of one's total development. Alfred North Whitehead [writes] that the major justification for a university is that "it maintains the connections between knowledge and the zest of life by uniting the young and the old in the imaginative consideration of learning." Considering our human physical-biological and emotional-intellectual-psychological endowments, I ask you if there is another discipline which can add so much to the "zest of life" as physical education?

("ROLE OF HISTORY AND PHILOSOPHY IN DETERMINING FUTURE DIRECTIONS IN PHYSICAL EDUCATION," *65th CPEA Proceedings,* 1962.)

THE SEEDBED OF CREATIVE ACTIVITY

*[Like so many young Americans, Billy Wireman was deeply
moved by President John Kennedy's evocation of a New
Frontier. Here, in this 1962 article, Dr. Wireman argues
that physical education, sports, recreation, and leisure ought
not be considered simply another form of passive consumption. Instead, he places sports and recreation in the context of
John Kennedy's New Frontier struggle for freedom.]*

I f the disciplines of physical education and recreation
do not seek to develop in people the concept that
recreation should be a creative, enriching experience,
then they have violated one of their fundamental responsibilities. We must all synthesize our talents with a common purpose which is to establish and perpetuate a lasting
world peace under international law—a peace in which
individuals have an opportunity to express their unique
personalities in the way each sees fit. Leisure and recreation can make a very distinct and valuable contribution
to this lofty aim by being the seedbed of creative activity.
Cultural mediocrity and moral degeneration are the inevi-
table results when leisure becomes nothing more than
merely time for vicarious participation and unlimited
consumption. The real index of the vitality of a society is

the degree to which the citizens become involved in that society's total business—involved as citizen-participants and not merely as citizen-consumers. Recreation, with its vast wholesome potential, is a vital part of our society's total business. It is therefore incumbent upon each of us to develop "worthy uses" for our "leisure time."

("RECREATION AND AMERICA'S
NATIONAL PURPOSE," *Peabody
Journal of Education*, JANUARY 1962.)

SEARCH IS AN ACTIVE VERB

[By 1964, Billy Wireman was thinking not only about physical education as technique, but physical education as part of moral education, as he explains below.]

Education is a search for enlightenment and understanding and meaning. All who seek diligently shall find. I would remind you that search is an active verb. This search is an ongoing process and must constantly be in pursuit of the unknown, the new experience, and must bring some reward to the person and must give the "searcher" confidence. The end result should be that time-worn cliché: the rich, full, abundant life.

Education should free the intellect from ignorance and make of it a critical but constructive instrument. Education should examine the moral and ethical dimensions of a student's life. Education should bring the student in contact with a possible life's vocation and should develop in each student the ability to express himself or herself creatively through the fine arts and some sport or hobby.

The underlying values of physical education should be apparent in these qualities:

• Being sensitive to the historical evolution of human feelings about physical education and physical activity.

• Being proficient in a leisure-time skill to the degree that the citizen will seek out this activity for relaxation and recreation.

• Having a body capable of sustaining itself in the daily demands made upon it.

• Understanding the concept of total health.

("What are the Underlying Values in Physical Education?" *Florida J.O.H.P.E.R.*, February 1964.)

Disappointment at the World's Fair

[By 1964, Billy Wireman had begun to think of education, not only physical education but education in general, as a kind of "soulcraft." No wonder that he was deeply disappointed by the 1964 World's Fair Pavilion on Education.]

It was with great anticipation that I looked forward to visiting the Hall of Education at the New York World's Fair. In preparing for my visit to the Fair, I remember discussing with a colleague the crucial role of education in a free society. My disappointment upon visiting the Hall of Education could not have been greater.

Rather than the story of American education, I found a crassly commercial hodge-podge of everything and anything and consequently nothing. Rather than a penetrating and moving explanation of the key role of public education in a free society, I found two restaurants, a bar, and several gift shops. Rather than a message in depth of how forty million young men and women each year are taught the skills necessary to function in a democratic social order, I found numerous commercial book displays, a place to have my handwriting analyzed, an invitation to buy a billiard table, a number of religious exhibits, an opportunity to participate in a chess tournament, and a display of machines and tools. But still I looked for the story of how American education seeks to release the full, creative potential of each individual. But still this story was not to be found. Indeed, further investigation revealed only that I could have my portrait painted for $5.00, order a cap and gown or a pair of tennis shoes, view a coin exhibit, rest in a lounge chair, or answer a request to "discuss your wall and floor problems with us."

Nowhere in the Pavilion did I find an emphasis on the importance of ideas, or an examination of the ingredients of creative teaching.

At a time when controversy swirls about what should be the content and direction of American education, it is sad indeed that this Pavilion represents what many critics say is the essence of American education: a disjointed, fragmented group of frills and gimmicks, with no depth, no cohesiveness, no organizing principle, no substance, no continuity.

("The Hall of Education at the
World's Fair: A Great Disappoint-
ment," *Peabody Journal of Education,*
September 1964.)

LISTEN IN ORDER TO LEARN

[If the World's Fair didn't exactly capture the essence of education, what is that essence then? In this 1965 article, Billy Wireman argued that a first mark of the educated person is an ability not so much to talk as to listen.]

One of the most difficult things for people to discipline themselves to do is to listen. We all think that what we have to say is important, simply because we're the ones who know it. So listening, which requires the discipline of removing yourself from the center of the stage, is an extremely difficult task.

The historian R. G. Collingwood stated that philosophy is reflective. It is thought of the second degree. When you think about what you have thought then you are philosophizing, so philosophy is a by-product of reflective thinking and listening. And how does this relate to education? Well, let's define our terms. Education is a search for enlightenment, understanding, and meaning. The individual seeks to become in actuality what he or she was only potentially—and this, of course, involves learning. Moving from the known to the unknown and back again gives confidence, and then moving back again into the unknown, building on what you have learned before, is the process of enlightenment. All of this learning emerges from struggle, coming into contact with what is unfamiliar to you, and then moving on from there, broadening your horizons.

Now, there are three types of listening which are necessary to this process. First of all, you have listening to yourself. Listen to yourself talk, think deeply, not superficially, and reach an understanding of your own potential so that you operate on the basis of your real self and not what someone else thinks you ought to be.

Then, of course, you have listening to others, detaching yourself from the basic human desire to be the center of the stage.

Then you have another kind of listening which, to me, is very important, and that is reading. Reading is a form of listening.

Let me add one word more. Seeing and observing is a form of listening, but the end result of this process is action. If we stop by developing just "theory," the great concept of combining the philosopher and the practical person into someone who gets things done may fail.

The closed mind is a dead mind. We must be receptive to new ideas and weigh each idea and each answer on the basis of merit and not prejudice. In order to get new ideas we must let the other fellow talk, and letting the other fellow talk, we must listen.

It would be difficult to imagine a more sophisticated

approach to human affairs than democracy. The whole concept of freedom is based on the assumption that people are not only politically free, economically free, religiously free, but also intellectually free. People are free, genuinely free, only to the degree that they have a rational and firm grasp of the major forces which operate around them. Free, only to the degree that they understand what is going on in the world today and relate themselves to that in a meaningful way.

("LISTENING—THE LOST ART OF EDUCATION," *The Toastmaster*, FEBRUARY 1965.)

Developing Carriers and Creators

[The World Fair's Hall of Education provoked Billy Wireman to think more vigorously about the aim of education. As a Kennedyesque "New Frontiersman," he was convinced that we must educate persons to be citizens, not simply employees. A "citizen" is a free person who lives with other free persons in a world of equals called a republic in which all can participate in the construction of their common future. Echoing an ancient tradition which goes back to the Greeks, Dr. Wireman insists in this 1965 article that humans can flourish only as citizens in a free and equal republic.]

On any given weekday morning between September and June, forty-five million young men and women attend primary and secondary schools in America to learn how to function effectively in a free society. Ours is the most gigantic, massive approach ever taken to educating a whole society.

The point of departure for this "education for freedom" must be an understanding of the deeper meanings of human existence. For, as Pindar held, the duty of education is to help us "become who we are." This duty implies that we are something to begin with and that growth occurs as this something is developed.

Jacques Maritain illustrates the seamless connection between education and a concept of humanity: "Education cannot escape the problems and entanglements of philosophy. For it supposes by its very nature a philosophy of man."

A society which believes in the principle of individual liberty must insist that its educational system reflects this belief. For education, in its broadest sense, is nothing more than a search for enlightenment and understanding and meaning. The result should be a citizen who is living the "examined," disciplined, balanced life. In developing this type of citizen, formal education should do the following:

• Free the intellect from ignorance and make of it a critical but constructive instrument. This can be done by developing in each student a firm grasp of what *has been* and *what is* and by asking *what ought to be?*

• Examine the moral and ethical dimension of each student's life.

• Bring the student in contact with a possible life's vocation.

• Develop in each student the ability to express himself or herself creatively.

Because the free citizen in a democratic state is both carrier and creator of his or her culture, democracy is the most sophisticated approach imaginable to human affairs. Intellectual risks must be taken, boldness and imagination are to be cherished, and a premium must be placed on new ideas. A free state must operate on the assumption that the truth is discoverable but not necessarily discovered.

Clearly there is a "seamless connection" between education, democracy, and the human condition.

("EDUCATION, DEMOCRACY, AND THE HUMAN CONDITION," *School and Society,* OCTOBER 16, 1965.)

The Power of Unarmed Truth

[What are the specific marks of the educated person, this "citizen"? Billy Wireman thought that commitment, the ability to spend your life for a cause worth a life, is a key virtue of the educated person and the citizen, as he explains in this Sunday school talk he gave in 1965, keyed to Acts 16:25-40.]

What would be our answer to the question, "What am I trying to do?" "What do I want the total of all my efforts to accomplish?" Is this too abstract? I think not. Indeed, until each individual establishes his or her basic commitment there is a great danger that vanity, pride, and selfishness will creep into his or her decisions. Unless each of us can answer the basic question, "What am I trying to do?" with a firm commitment that all of our efforts are devoted to bring about the common good through wisdom, justice, Christian love, and tolerance, then our efforts are likely to be undisciplined and misguided. We would never want to confuse unity of purpose with unanimity of opinion or approach, but under our collective efforts there must be a common denominator which attempts to bring a contemporary Christ to a contemporary world with contemporary problems. The point is clear and I repeat it again for emphasis:

God works through us. God gave us dominion over the earth and God expects us to accept the responsibilities inherent in this power. What has moved people down through the ages? Not the cudgel. Not the sword. But the irresistible power of unarmed truth.

("COMMITMENT," *Adult Uniform Lessons*, FALL 1965.)

The College's Central Objective

[Education itself is a kind of commitment, or even more strongly, a kind of "calling"; it is not simply a profession or career. Education engages teachers and students in the profound challenge of creating new worlds. Education is about the past, and the preservation of what's good and the extirpation of what's evil; it's about the present; and it's especially about the future, about sowing seeds for fruits that the teacher may never even see. In 1965, when he himself was the chief development officer at Florida Presbyterian College, Dr. Wireman discussed the professional qualifications of the people at colleges who struggle to raise money, but insists on the moral dimension of the development officer's duties.]

The recent Danforth Commission preliminary report on church colleges and universities in the United States entitled *Eight Hundred Colleges Face the Future* lists four basic trends in American society, two of which should be of concern to every person even remotely interested in the church-related college.

One trend the study detected is the progressive secularization of western culture and a decline in the effectiveness of the church. Another is the deterioration of the position of liberal arts education in the United States during the last century. If these trends are to be arrested, we must somehow find dedicated, capable, imaginative, knowledgeable people who will go into college development, not because it offers an opportunity to make more money, or to "sell education," but because they feel this is the way they can best serve the cause of their church and country.

Henry Wriston, writing in *Academic Procession,* lists two basic rules of college administration. First, he says college administrators must realize that they do not have a "product" but they exist to develop people. Secondly, and growing out of this basic truth, is the fact that the machinery through which a college achieves its ends is composed of people. Wriston further sharpens the nature of a college by stating that its "central objective is the cultivation of the mind." Development officers who accept this basic truth and can relate its significance to possible sources of support are priceless. Those who do not, however well-intentioned they might be, are doomed to failure. This is as it should be.

("Raison D'être," *College and University Journal,* Fall 1965.)

The Idea of Freedom's Time

[For Billy Wireman, even informal, everyday duties, like speaking to a Girl Scouts gathering, could be an occasion to think aloud about his passion, education. Here are some remarks he made to Florida scouts in 1966.]

I hope you agree with me today that it is a great and exciting time. There will be no nuclear war. Communism is not the way of the future. The historic struggle of all people to reach a level of meaningful existence will slowly but surely be won. We are in a great revolution. But the most revolutionary idea of all is that we can be free, that we can make a better life. The historian Charles Beard saw "the establishment of a regime of liberty over a vast region," as America's most significant contribution to the advancement of civilization. Victor Hugo observed that "all the treading armies are less mighty than an idea whose time has come." So let us continue today the common task of proving that "the idea of freedom's time" has come.

("Not By Talent Alone," *Vital Speeches of the Day*, April 1, 1966.)

A Vacuum Begging to be Filled

[Profoundly shaped by John Kennedy's New Frontier, Billy Wireman, as a young college president, had to confront the turmoil of the 1960s. On his first day in office, he jokes, student protesters demanded that he end racism in America and the war in Vietnam. Though not uncritical of the 1960s protesters, Dr. Wireman saw the student turbulence of the 1960s as a response to the universities' failures of vision. More and more universities had become fragmented; more and more the educational process had become less human and more bureaucratic. Here is Dr. Wireman's commentary on the early wave of student protest.]

All across the land we are seeing turbulence and unrest on college and university campuses. They represent an outward manifestation of a deeper trend in higher education toward dehumanizing the educational process and fragmenting the educational experience. This is a severe indictment of educational leadership for failing to give the university what Robert Hutchins calls a "vision of its own end." Rather than having a "vision" and being a living, pulsating organism with a soul, a personality, and an identity of its own, the university has disintegrated into disjointed, frustrated groups of vested interests, each pursuing its own selfish goals, with little regard for its total mission.

The center of controversy in this disintegration of the university concept has been the student.

The faculty member is caught between the demands of research, writing, consulting and teaching.

The administration, not really knowing what higher education is trying to do, finds itself more and more performing a public relations function of attempting to interpret the university to a skeptical public.

The result is the university becomes a legal entity only, pulled and stretched almost beyond recognition. Because it has no organizing principle, no unity, no cutting edge, no cohesiveness, inevitably there exists at the heart of the university a great collective vacuum—a vacuum begging to be filled with a dynamic, relevant, coordinated program, administered by concerned human beings who are genuinely interested in seeking and claiming the truth.

Rather than the historic concept of the university as "the ancient and universal company of scholars," we have what Hutchins has called "a series of separate schools and departments held together by a central heating system." Clark Kerr, president of the University of California, describes the modern university as a "mechanism held together by administrative rules and powered by money."

In solving these problems, we must first agree that the main purpose of higher education is to provide a relevant and rewarding educational experience for the undergraduate student. Only as the university changes the student's attitudes and behavior in a positive and constructive manner, as the student unfolds intellectually and morally, does the university fulfill its historic function.

This brings us to the second critical weakness of the modern university—teaching. We must place a premium on, and further reward, great teaching.

Only by restoring the primacy of teaching and making the university a "living organism" with an integrity of its own can we arrest the debilitating trends toward dehumanization and fragmentation.

("Student Turbulence An Indictment of the Universities," *St. Petersburg Times*, April 16, 1966.)

The Alchemy of Human Knowledge

[The student protests of the 1960s infuriated and confused millions of Americans. As a college administrator, Dr. Wireman became a kind of translator between people within the academy and those without. What should citizens know about education? At least three things, he thought, as outlined in this 1967 article.]

The first thing is to understand the nature of a college. A college should be, in Walter Lippmann's words, "a laboratory, where alchemists work, transmuting human knowledge into human wisdom; wisdom reshaped to human scale and human understanding." So, an educational institution is more than a transmitter of knowledge. In its broadest sense, it is a search for enlightenment.

Another important point to understand is the role of dissent in a free society. The role of dissent and questioning, so vital to the progress of the business community, unfortunately has never been fully accepted and understood in the area of education.

Lastly citizens should know how to evaluate the educational process. Citizens should ask: "What should be taught—to whom and to what end?" A lack of philosophic depth is one of the great shortcomings of American higher education.

("Do Politics, Education Mix?" *St. Petersburg Independent*, February 11, 1967.)

Understanding the Nature of Learning

[Far from being frightened by the turmoil on America's campuses, Billy Wireman thought the turmoil could be turned to good.]

At long last, the university and American society are engaged in a heated but meaningful dialogue about the purposes of education. This dialogue, sparked by student demonstrations, is producing many tensions which are fraught with both potential for good and danger of great harm.

Most of the troublesome problems facing higher education stem from a basic lack of understanding about the nature of the learning process itself. All learning emerges from struggle. Struggle means conflict.

A meaningful educational experience involves students intellectually and emotionally in the conflicts of their culture and asks them to formulate some judgments as to how these conflicts might be resolved.

Growing out of this basic nature of the learning experience is another source of tension: a failure to understand the critical role of dissent in a free society.

Another source of tension is failure to understand how the academic community governs itself. "Community" is the key word here, and the vitality of this community depends upon the degree to which each element—trustees, faculty, administration, and students—feels an emotional and intellectual stake in establishing the direction and purpose of the institution. Academic governance, consequently, rests upon the decentralization of power. The university president is considered the intellectual leader of the academic community, a "first among equals." The president's relationship is not one of employer-employee but rather colleague to colleague.

What is especially called for here is an inexhaustible supply of mutual respect.

("FPC Leader Discusses Concern of Public for Educational Purposes," *Vision*, March 1967.)

The Essence of Responsible Citizenship

[The 1960s events—the student protests, the Civil Rights movement, the Vietnam War—all threw into question, at least for some Americans, the kind of deep patriotism which so moved Billy Wireman. Yet these struggles to reform America only confirmed Dr. Wireman's patriotism, as he explains in this 1967 speech honoring astronaut Edward White, who had just been killed in a training accident.]

Astronaut White's tragic and untimely death serves to remind us all of the tenuousness of life and the abruptness with which it can be snuffed out. It serves to remind us all that in the final analysis we will be judged on the questions: "What did we do with what we had?" "How did we choose to use those talents with which we were endowed?" To me, Ed White's life represents a noble strain in the unfolding human drama which should inspire each of us. To me, he represents the same pioneering spirit which has been prevalent through American history.

What were the virtues key to the pioneering adventure? They were strength of will; the depth of determination; the ability to negotiate a hostile environment; an ability to maintain perspective in times of misfortune and tragedy; and a determination to keep your eyes fixed on greater goal ahead.

Every generation must win anew the battle of human liberty. And in fighting this battle, there are always new frontiers to conquer.

There is a strange and sinister sort of mood loose in American today. Somehow patriotism has become suspect. And so an important question for each of us is: What kind of America do we want? Will we continue to stand for those noble principles which guided Ed White, or will we become captives of the forces of hate and radicalism?

I, for one, feel that we must keep America strong. And this can be done only by developing in each citizen the capacity to return enlightened judgments—the capacity to interpret a meaningful patriotism—the capacity to stand for unpopular causes—the capacity, when principle is involved, to be a minority of one, remembering always the wellspring of our national commitment found in the *Declaration of Independence*: "All men are created equal, with certain inalienable rights, among these are life, liberty, and the pursuit of happiness." This is not a plea for a blind and arrogant patriotism. I am calling for a patriotism based on conviction, and pride, and respect for our fellow citizens.

We should want people to be attracted to our way of doing things, not because we are Americans, but because we are free. We should want others to be impressed with us, not for the glitter of our wealth, but for the splendor of our ideals.

Now, a person is genuinely free only when he or she is free to investigate, to criticize, and to question ideas because ideas are the forces which energize history.

This is the essence of responsible citizenship: living the kind of life that a free society deserves and demands, returning enlightened, informed, responsible judgments on the key issues of the day; getting involved as a participant in those things which are dear to you and working to bring about your ideas; being the kind of citizen who, in the words of Abraham Lincoln, is "principled, but not fanatic; who is flexible, but not opportunistic; who is ambitious, but not ruthless; resigned but not passive." In short, a citizen who is excited by the concept of freedom but who understands clearly that freedom is not free. It is almost trite to call ours a revolutionary age, but by any standard it is indeed. But the most revolutionary idea of all is still that people can be free.

("A Tribute to Astronaut Edward
H. White," unpublished speech, June
5, 1967.)

PROFILE OF A VOLUNTEER

[By 1968, Billy Wireman had become the youngest college president in America. His days were taken up with the inexhaustible flow of day-to-day academic busyness. But no matter how mundane the chore, Wireman approached it with a much wider vision in mind. College presidents, especially presidents of small, independent colleges, depend on cadres of volunteers, and one of a president's central jobs is to recruit, retain, and inspire such volunteers. Here, in this 1967 article, Dr. Wireman describes the kind of volunteer he hoped to rally to the cause of Florida Presbyterian College. His portrait of the ideal volunteer, though, is embedded in his vision of the educated person and committed citizen. It is also, his friends would add, a striking self-portrait.]

At the heart of every great movement in history has been a core of advocates who, in the face of overwhelming odds, have determined that their cause would succeed. That is true in the development of America. It is true in the development of the church. It is true for my institution.

As we sketch out the profile of a volunteer, let us focus first on the fact that he or she is a person, a real live human being, with all the characteristics inherent in the human condition. When we get caught up in our intense desire to "win the campaign," we sometimes expect the volunteer to be something that we are not—a highly efficient, highly reliable, almost machine-like individual who can cause miracles to happen simply by pressing buttons. But humans are just not like that.

All of us have four basic wishes: the desire for recognition, the desire for response, the desire for security, and the desire for new experience.

It is important to remember that more than likely a volunteer will react emotionally to questions and then rationalize his or her response. A person takes in a fact, relates this fact to what he or she already knows, then acts on the basis of some commitment. Like all human beings a volunteer has a set of values—a "hot line," if you please—something that is extremely dear and personally important. It follows, therefore, that getting to know volunteers and finding out what makes them tick is absolutely essential.

The second characteristic of this volunteer is that this person represents some form of power. This power might be financial, it might be political. It might center in church and religious circles. One of the original sins in development is the misuse of volunteers—asking them to do tasks they are not prepared to accomplish.

Power often (though by no means always!) accrues to able people. Thus this volunteer is, more than likely, a very able person, who can accept challenges, who appreciates no small talk, who is not deceived about how easy the task will be, who can rise to great purposes, and who desires to be in a situation where the outcome is important.

The ideal volunteer is extremely busy and is not looking for additional assignments. He or she will not be impressed with fuzzy ideas or mushy goals. This ideal volunteer is well-organized and operates on a tight schedule; our ideal person typically will be punctual, brief, and concise.

Our volunteer solves problems. Vague abstractions and fuzzy commitments to excellence leave the volunteer cold. This person wants facts, figures, and plans. He or she likes to, and must, get things done—to move problems from the theoretical to the real—to make decisions. To coordinate these decisions, and then move on to other decisions. Action the volunteer must have.

Human beings react viscerally rather than cerebrally to philosophic issues. We all have something we hold dear; we all care intensely, emotionally, almost irrationally about something. Because of this, our ideal volunteer can and should be inspired, moved by noble purposes. It is noble purposes and personal commitment, and not simply arguments and reasons, that powerfully move people. This is why the old plant trees and the young die in wars—this ability to remove one's self from the temporal and ephemeral to work for the lasting and enduring.

So here is our ideal volunteer—someone powerful, able, busy, well-organized, a problem-solver, someone who can accept great challenges, who craves inspiration and excitement, who, if really inspired, will gladly make a sacrificial gift. Let us not bother such a person with small tasks. Instead, let us confront such a person with some great challenge which only such people can meet.

("PROFILE OF A VOLUNTEER," *College and University Journal*, SUMMER 1967.)

Connecting "Liberal" and "Arts"

[The answer to America's 1960s confusion was education, Billy Wireman thought, an education for citizenship. Citizenship was central to Billy Wireman's vision of education. Citizenship arose, he increasingly argued, from active engagement with the liberal arts, particularly the liberal arts education students can receive at a small, church-related college. "Liberal arts" is a kind of metaphor: it links two quite different things together. "Arts" refer to the specific skills one needs to have a "productive career" within the specific framework of the "here and now." "Liberal" refers, though, to opening the mind and heart to other worlds and other possibilities, to the investigation of past worlds, or future worlds, or dream worlds. "Liberal" and "arts" must remain connected if educators are, as Martha Nussbaum writes, to "cultivate humanity." This is the point Dr. Wireman makes in this 1967 speech.]

Liberal education is about the education of *persons*. Education should be a search, a search for enlightenment. But is this the kind of education college students are receiving today? All across the country we are seeing protests by students who are disenchanted with the dehumanized, depersonalized education they are receiv-

ing. Education must be on a human-to-human relationship, and all of the techniques in the world cannot supply
this important ingredient. The element of humanity can
only be supplied by humans, by individuals.

("The Man Behind the Word," *Vital
Speeches of the Day*, September 1, 1967.)

Contrast of Haves and Have-Nots

[It has become a truism that education must be global. But this was no truism in the 1960s. It was very much a new idea, and indeed Billy Wireman was one of education's early "globalists." Over the years, he was an educational consultant to a variety of worldwide organizations, and again and again he insisted that global vision was integral to a coherent education. As part of an international consultation mission, Dr. and Mrs. Wireman, in October 1967, set off on a 32,000-mile, 15-country trip around the world.]

I t was "the best of times, it was the worst of times." This quote from Dickens occurred to me repeatedly during our trip. The best of times we found in the western societies where the standards of living and conveniences were much as we would find them in America. The worst of times we found in the unbelievable condition of the majority of people in Asia. The contrast between the "have" and "have-not" nations was brought into very sharp focus during this trip.

("Our Trip Around the World," unpublished speech, October 1967.)

Money Isn't Everything for Schools

[After thirty-plus years as a college president, Billy Wireman often jokes that his day job has been to raise roughly $10,000 per day, day in and day out, year in and year out. Private schools, like private businesses, survive by their financial wits. Typically they have little fat to fall back on; a single major blunder can destroy a private school. Their leaders must not only balance the budget but raise the revenue, and Dr. Wireman has spent a lifetime wooing givers, running fundraising campaigns, and sweating over budgets. He has been astonishingly successful. At Queens College, for example, the endowment increased tenfold during his tenure. And yet, for all its importance, Dr. Wireman has consistently warned that "money isn't everything." In 1968, for example, Dr. Wireman waded into a local argument about a "financial crisis" then facing Florida's public schools.]

Make no mistake—money is important. But it is a condition, rather than a guarantee, of high-quality schools. Education of true and lasting excellence will come when, and only when, enlightened and courageous schools boards demand dynamically relevant and academically vital schools staffed by competent and concerned teachers and administrators.

Citizens, therefore, who want to ensure that the money will be spent wisely should ask the Legislature to institute three specific changes in the present educational structure.

The first has to do with the method of electing school board members. The decisive factor at present in school board races is a candidate's political party. Unfortunately, but inescapably, this discourages many qualified candidates from seeking election to the board.

There is no rational justification for electing school board members on a partisan basis. There is no "party line" in education. So, if the Legislature is serious about wanting to make Florida "first in education" it will remove school board elections from partisan politics.

The second reform should be in restructuring the administrative staff in the public school to reflect that this is in fact a place where serious scholarship and learning takes place. The typical public school has a principal, a dean of men, a dean of women, a host of counselors, a registrar, a director of athletics, a business manager, and many other supportive administrative positions. Conspicuously absent in the typical public school is an administrator whose prime responsibility is the academic program.

The third and perhaps the most controversial area where considerable improvement could be made is in teacher evaluation. The idea that teaching cannot be evaluated must be dismissed. Robert G. Aldous, school official of Ogden, Utah, hits on two key points. One, teachers must be involved in instituting any evaluation plan; and two, teacher salaries will remain at a fairly low level until some concept of incentive is built into raises and promotions. Good teachers would view a periodic evaluation not as a threat but as an opportunity to become more effective.

It is a time in America when "protest hangs heavy in the air." James Reston calls the present conflict "a crisis of the spirit." If we are to solve this crisis and prevent democracy's deadliest enemies—cynicism and disillusionment—from sapping the vitality of American society, then we must find a way to instill in our young a confidence in the future. This can be accomplished best through a strong and viable public school system.

("SCHOOLS: MONEY ISN'T EVERYTHING,"
St. Petersburg Times, JANUARY 21, 1968.)

A Process of Becoming

[Engaged constantly in fundraising and day-to-day management, Billy Wireman remained actively involved in discussions about the wider purposes of education. He was struck, for example, by the fluid nature of the educational process, by its dynamic, unpredictable, and sometimes even chaotic nature.]

I've written that education ought to be a kind of search, a search for enlightenment. "Search" is an active verb and implies some initiative on the part of the "searcher." Education, then, is an encounter—an encounter with one's self, one's fellow, one's God. It is an attempt to find meaning and purpose in the human enterprise and live out one's life in commitment.

Education is a process of "becoming." A person never "is" but is always in the state of "becoming."

This is a thoughtful, agonizing, often painful, but important experience. What is certain today is less certain tomorrow. Question and debate, criticism and disagreement are important elements in this process. Undergirding this whole process must be a commitment to the larger whole—to the broader human traditions of free institutions and evolutionary growth and respect for the rights of others. In short, an understanding that with freedom comes responsibility.

("Statement to Florida Presbyterian College," unpublished, May 1, 1968.)

A Community of Scholars

[At Florida Presbyterian College, Dr. Wireman, then the youngest college president in the United States, was an enthusiastic advocate of educational reform. He was convinced that the tumult on American college campuses was triggered at least in part by the failures of higher education to address students' most fundamental needs. In a long memorandum to his faculty, in May 1968, President Wireman called for the creation of three unique units at Florida Presbyterian, an "experimental college," an "inter-disciplinary college," and a "motivational college." In this memo, Dr. Wireman outlined his hopes and plans.]

The future of our college depends upon the degree to which we can maintain a relatively small, close-knit, economically viable, academically vital, human community, where individuals can relate on a person-to-person basis, where human problems and concerns will get human responses. Unfortunately, the trend in American society is increasingly for interlocking forces to dehumanize and fragment our daily existence. This trend has worked its way into the academic community, especially at the large universities. We are seeing some ugly manifestations of this problem across the country now at some of our larger universities. Subtle but powerful forces will set in here for fragmentation and depersonalization if we are not cautious. We simply must not permit this to happen.

Preserving a human, concerned community will necessitate that we remain as small as possible without being economically unfeasible.

Time in education is extremely important. We do not know very much about learning, but we do know that perhaps second only to religious experience, the educational experience is the most personal of all human experiences. This requires a thoughtful, reflective process which can best take place in a more intimate complex of people.

The attitude necessary for keeping a community human is much more easily developed in a smaller community where conversation and dialogue can take place within the disciplines and among students, faculty, the church, trustees, and administrators. Smaller communities make it possible to know more members of the community. Purposes can be discussed and shared and criticized and agreed upon at deeper levels. With bigness inevitably comes bureaucratic centralization with a centripetal force toward the center. This too tends to dehumanize. And lost, then, is the whole idea of a "community of scholars."

The major assumption underlying the Experimental College is that *every time we teach someone something we deny him or her the privilege and thrill of learning it independently.* Thus, in the Experimental College there would be a heavy, almost exclusive emphasis on independent study and the only limitation on its curriculum would be the boldness, imagination, ability, industry, and creativity of the students and professors involved. While I do not often agree with Paul Goodman, in the May edition of *Saturday Review* he spells out beautifully the concept behind the Experimental College:

> Unless there is a reaching from within, learning cannot become "second nature." It seems stupid to decide *a priori* what the young ought to know and then to try to motivate them, instead of letting the initiative come from them and putting information and relevant equipment at their service. Freedom is the only way toward authentic citizenship. Free choice is not random but responsive to real situations; both youth and adults live in a nature of things, a polity and an ongoing society, and it is these that attract interest and channel need. If the young, as they mature, can follow their bent and choose their topics, times, and teachers, and if teachers teach what they themselves consider important—which is all they can skillfully teach anyway—the needs of society will be adequately met; there will be more lively, independent, and inventive people; and in the fairly short run there will be a more sensible and efficient society.

A second college would be the interdisciplinary college. A major assumption of this college would be that meaningful and effective education involves the student in an experience which is constantly seeking relationships. The dialogue would center around what Crane Brinton calls "the big questions: life, destiny, right, truth, and God." The student in this college would encounter the world and its conflicts in its totality and complexity, and seek to develop a sense of wholeness in an age of increasing specialization. The heart of this college would be an interdisciplinary core experience.

I call the third college a "motivational college." This college would be geared for the underprivileged, disadvantaged student. Psychological security and reinforcement would be key elements in the student's experience. We would attempt to lift the disadvantaged out of the restrictive forces which have held them back. We would truly seek to "empower the intellect." We can talk all we want about attempting to correct some of the injustices in American society, but our mission as an educational institution is to do something about them at the substantive level. We can render no more important service as a Christian institution than to help these disadvantaged youngsters.

("Memorandum to the FPC Faculty," May 17, 1968.)

STUMBLING FROM CRISIS TO CRISIS

[The student protests of the 1960s inspired Billy Wireman to reflect critically on the practice of American higher education. What he saw did not impress him. However misguided the student protesters might be, they were, he thought, on to something, as he writes in this year-end report from Florida Presbyterian College, for 1968-1969.]

The year 1968-69 saw the crisis in American higher education deepen. Violence resulted in the breakdown of internal order on many campuses. While the reasons for this crisis are many and complex, there is increasing agreement that higher education is plagued with many deep-seated problems which stem from failure to institute long-overdue academic reforms. The major problem is an inability to deal with the sheer size of the enterprise. Big universities have gotten bigger. Valuable resources are drained by graduate programs and a multiplicity of purposes; fragmentation has set in, and all too often the undergraduate experience is impoverished, at a time when the student is begging for, indeed demanding, a more relevant and rewarding undergraduate experience. It is more important now than ever that we bring the precision of the professor and the passion of the young into a mutually enriching relationship. The combination of bigness, fragmentation, and dehumanization has left much of higher education unmanageable in both human and educational terms. The result is that colleges and universities are on the verge of "imminent impotency" or, as one observer put it, "in a state of mindless and inefficient stumbling from crisis to crisis."

(*President's Report,* FLORIDA
PRESBYTERIAN COLLEGE, 1968-1969.)

Declare War on Ancient Enemies

[On March 8, 1969, Billy O. Wireman was formally inaugurated as the second president of Florida Presbyterian College. In his remarks, Dr. Wireman summarized the key themes to his vision of higher education.]

We meet today to exercise the principle that free men and women who believe in a benevolent God can join in common endeavor and build—a principle which has resulted in Florida Presbyterian College coming from dream to reality in ten short years. We meet to reflect upon a free institution in a free society.

Worldwide we are seeing the emancipation of persons from ancestral orders. We live in a world that is half-dead and half-born—a world caught between a war that can't be fought and a peace that can't be won—a world locked in a senseless and exorbitantly expensive arms race, but a world in which two-thirds of its people will go to bed hungry—a world twenty minutes away from nuclear annihilation, but seemingly light years away from human justice. We live in one, single, vulnerable, human community, with the capacity to destroy ourselves.

In American we find one of the last best hopes for

persons to participate actively and decisively in their own affairs, but festering throughout America's spectacular economic and industrial growth have been nagging and persistent problems too long delayed.

We must reflect on the nature of the university. Universities are unique in the family of human institutions. A university is not a microcosm of the larger society where decisions are made by popular vote. Neither is it, in its strictest sense, a private corporation where decisions are made at the top and handed down. The university is a learning community—a community which seeks its ends not in profits or political victories but in human terms. By bringing human potentiality into human actuality, it releases the full creative potential of people and develops in them the capacity to become enlightened, responsible, productive citizens—citizens able to sustain and enrich a free social order.

The chemistry for educational significance is involving bright students with able professors in programs dealing with real issues. This is the stuff of which educational vitality is made. In the past in education, we have absorbed too many facts and thought about them too little. Through pedagogical imagination we must invest facts with their possibilities and join the romantic idealism of the young with the precision of the professor in a relationship which is mutually enriching and fulfilling.

William James once called for the moral equivalent of

war. Let us declare war on humanity's ancient and historic enemies—intolerance, injustice, prejudice, ignorance, hunger, disease, poverty—and devote our efforts to removing "tyranny from the mind of man" wherever it exists. There is a battle being waged this morning for the very soul of humanity. When the beast in us is all too apparent, let us build a monument to the best in us. Let us cast this college's lot irrevocably with those enlightened, just, and humane people who want to build an enlightened, just, and humane society—a society which is known, not for the glitter of its wealth, but for the splendor of its ideas— a society which heeds the warning of the ancient scriptures: "Where there is no vision, the people perish."

("Formulating a New Trust: Inaugural Remarks," MARCH 8, 1969.)

LINCHPINS OF A FREE SOCIETY

[Faced with the continuing crisis on America's campuses, Dr. Wireman argued that universities had to undergo major reforms, that the key reforms were neither managerial nor budgetary but spiritual, and that re-affirming academic integrity was a top priority.]

The breakdown of order on many university campuses forces us to ask: "Can the university govern itself?" One thing is sure, either the university will govern itself, or others will administer its affairs. Rational inquiry cannot thrive in an atmosphere of supercharged emotionalism. We in education have so long been concerned with reforming society at large, that we have failed to institute long overdue reform within.

A university must be, in its broadest sense, society thinking. Unique among human institutions, it depends upon those two linchpins of a free society—risk and trust. It asks each person to risk something for the good of the whole, which requires that we learn to trust one another.

And so we arrive at the key element in any human institution—integrity. Integrity means that trustees will establish policies in the public interest, and not be influenced by petty and uninformed criticism; that administrators be servants and use limited funds efficiently and productively; that faculty teach honestly, openly, and exercise academic freedom responsibly; that students abide by a code of honor and approach the academic enterprise with persistence and diligence.

("Prerequisites for Campus Integrity," *The Presbyterian Outlook*, March 31, 1969.)

OF POETS AND ARCHITECTS

[How shall we define the university? This is one of Billy Wireman's favorite definitions. He included it in the Florida Presbyterian College Handbook *for 1969-1970. It nicely articulates themes central to Dr. Wireman's educational vision.]*

Alfred North Whitehead said: "The justification for a university is that it preserves the connection between knowledge and the zest of life, by uniting the young and the old in the imaginative consideration of learning. The university imparts information, but it imparts it imaginatively. This atmosphere of excitement, arising from imaginative consideration, transforms knowledge. A fact is no longer a bare fact; it is invested with all its possibilities. It is no longer a burden on the memory; it is 'energising' as the poet of our dreams and as the architect of our purposes."

(*Florida Presbyterian College Handbook* FOR 1969-1970.)

BUILDING AUTHORITY FROM WITHIN

["Question Authority!" was one of the slogans of the 1960s, and Billy Wireman, as a young college president, found himself in the awkward position of the authority being questioned. He increasingly came to see in the 1960s a kind of "crisis of authority," or, as others would phrase it, a "crisis of legitimacy." People obey authorities because they more or less accept that authority as "legitimate." But situations arise when people, at least some people, question the legitimacy of their institutions, and the result is a fundamental crisis of authority. How should Americans deal with it? This is what was on Dr. Wireman's mind in this fall 1970 article.]

One of the defining characteristics of our age is the increasing intensity of a universal theme of history: the generational crisis. Too often we react unimaginatively and timidly to the outward manifestations of this age-old conflict, and fail to come to grips with the taproot of the problem, the widespread crisis in authority.

Evidence abounds that this crisis runs very deep, and centers around participation rather than independence. Indeed, who can doubt that the African American, taxpayer, consumer, soldier, worshiper in the pew, retiree, member of the clergy, all have joined the young in asking sometimes militantly for more participation in making decisions which affect them?

A combination of an instant information environment, the dizzying disorientation of change, and the unwillingness of adults to interpret the reasons for things being as they are, prompts Max Ways, in a *Fortune* article, "More Power to Everybody," to assert that: "The general trend of twentieth-century society, particularly in the U.S., is toward a wider distribution of power, a broadening of participation by individuals in controlling their own lives and work."

The major challenge facing American society is to build institutions that young and old alike can trust. Rather than continue with the sterile discussion of the Establishment versus the Non-Establishment, let us debate the real issue: How do we build a just, enlightened, and humane society? Then, at least, we will be talking about the right issue.

Authority is extremely important. But rather than being imposed wholly from without, authority in the future must be more freely given from within. Ensuring that this transition takes place within a trusting, healthy, constructive context is clearly the mandate of our time.

("CRISIS IN AUTHORITY," *College & University Journal*, FALL 1970.)

To Rebuild Confidence in Education

[If people are to respect educational institutions and educators' authority, then educators must articulate clearly and compellingly just what they can and cannot do. The failure to do this was, Billy Wireman thought, part of the crisis of the universities in the 1960s and 1970s.]

After a brief respite, university and public-school administrators have welcomed record enrollments, eight million in higher education and fifty million in public schools.

Though the surface and immediate problems range from campus unrest to dorm hours for the university, and busing and dress codes for the public schools, educators at all levels must soon come to grips with a more serious and pressing problem: the massive loss of public confidence in American education. This unfortunate development stems basically from the stubborn unwillingness or more probably the tragic inability of educators to articulate a simple, compelling, and clearly understood rationale for education. The truth is that no one seems to know what education is supposed to do, much less how it is supposed to do it.

In determining the basis upon which educators should

be held accountable, I suggest that education should attempt to:

- Free the intellect from ignorance and make of it a critical but constructive instrument. This can be done by developing in each student a firm grasp of what "has been" and "what is" and by asking the student to call on his or her own resources to state "what ought to be."
- Examine the moral dimension of a student's life and encourage him or her to develop a clear and compelling set of personal values.
- Bring the student in contact with a possible life's vocation.
- Develop the student's ability to express himself or herself creatively.

("EDUCATORS DON'T KNOW WHAT EDUCATION SHOULD DO," *The National Observer*, OCTOBER 5, 1970.)

Four Characteristics of a Just Society

[Dr. Wireman, in the 1960s and 1970s, was a committed patriot, and an impatient reformer. In December 1970, he spoke to the senior class at the University of Tampa. He argued that serious reform was essential in American institutions, including, indeed especially, the university.]

Our institutions must be reformed to genuinely serve the people for whom they exist. As we meet this demand for reform, let us return to four characteristics of a just, enlightened, and humane society:

• A belief in the worth, dignity, and sacredness of the human personality. As you seek to renew and repair America, place this commitment at the top of your priorities. Every anti-human force must be removed.

• The dignity, worth, and sacredness of the human personality can best be enhanced through a free and ordered society wherein people can participate actively and decisively in their own affairs. Democracy is the form of government most consistent with a belief in the sacredness of the human person. But democracy does not guarantee good government. Democracy assumes much on the part of the individual citizen. When is a person genuinely free? I would suggest to you that a person is genuinely free only when he or she is legally, politically, economically, religiously, and educationally free, free from ignorance and prejudice and economic reprisal, and thus has the resources to manage his or her own life and work free from the domination of others. We must begin to educate for total freedom or abandon the idea.

• If the human person is sacred and of ultimate worth, and we have prepared the citizen to reach full potential, it therefore follows that a respect for diversity and pluralism is a key characteristic of the America of the future.

• Finally, the new America requires a respect for the importance of the critical mind. We must operate on the assumption that the truth is discoverable but not necessarily discovered, thus continually question the fundamental assumptions under which we are operating.

Every generation must win and re-win human freedom. You are heirs to a rich cultural heritage. You inherit the most promising experiment ever undertaken in establishing a regime of liberty over a vast continent. But America never "is." America is always in a state of "becoming."

("AMERICA REVISITED," *Remarks to the Graduating Class of Tampa University,* DECEMBER 20, 1970.)

SOMEONE QUESTIONED THE STATUS QUO

[The United States' impending birthday, in 1976, inspired everyone to think about America's meanings. For Billy Wireman, the 1976 Bicentennial was an occasion to urge educators to "educate for freedom," as he writes in this 1973 article.]

L et's not forget that America came into being because someone questioned the status quo and had an attitude of skepticism and healthy irreverence. If we forget our revolutionary beginnings now, and deny that all we have as we face the future is human intelligence and human wisdom applied compassionately, boldly, imaginatively, to human problems, then we would have made a colossal error in judgment about the fundamental needs of human freedom. And human freedom, I emphasize, is what America is all about. We must, in short, either begin to educate for freedom or abandon the idea.

("How to Restore Confidence in Education," *St. Petersburg Times*, September 23, 1973.)

THE DEFENSE AGAINST BAD IDEAS

[The mid-1970s were a time for retrospection, as the Bicentennial approached, but also a time for dreaming of the future, as Americans felt the strange sensation that the millennium was approaching. Thinking of the future, it was the relationship between ideas and institutions which remained central to Billy Wireman's thought. A scholar himself, fascinated by the world of ideas, he was also a manager and leader, charged with organizing and leading a growing educational institution. Connecting (another of his favorite words) ideas to action was a recurring theme, as in this 1974 article.]

As we look to the last third of the twentieth century and beyond, we simply must bring into being a new coalition among power, principles, and ideas. The greatest deficiency in the human enterprise at this time is the lack of capacity to take new and promising ideas and make them manifest in institutional structures which deal with people on the basis of sound human political and ethical principles.

The only defense against bad ideas is good ideas. The wildest dream is the first step to reality. Let us catch a vision of a better society and then seek to bring that society about. Everything begins with an idea. It can begin no-where else. In the future, human intelligence, applied boldly, sympathetically, imaginatively to human problems is our only hope.

"Liberty," said Judge Learned Hand, "lies in the hearts of men and women and when it dies there, no parliament, no court, no edict, no constitution, can restore it."

("'JONATHAN' MUST RETURN TO EARTH," *St. Petersburg Times,* JUNE 9, 1974.)

A Declaration of Education

[In 1976, as part of the nation's ongoing Bicentennial reflection, Billy Wireman proposed a "Declaration of Education." It was published in 1977.]

I propose, in the Bicentennial spirit, the 1976 Declaration of Education. The greatest deficiency at all levels of education in America is the absence of clearcut statements of objectives to which the Academy has committed itself and which non-educators can understand. We educators too often talk to ourselves and disregard the wider community.

And so, I propose the following:

The Academy is a learning community committed to a learning society.

Its principal business being learning, the Academy seeks, primarily but not exclusively through the life of the mind, to liberate human beings into an authentic and effective personhood by engaging them in a lifelong learning experience characterized by rigor, flexibility, and a concern for human, democratic, and moral values.

Authenticity implies identity, genuineness, integrity, self-respect, honesty, and the capacity to care. Effectiveness means more than competence. Inherent in effectiveness is knowing how to learn, to do, to manage, to execute—in short, to be.

The skills necessary to maintain oneself in a lifelong learning experience are found in the mutual interaction and relative dominance of four basic learning units: learning to learn; learning to do; learning to care; and learning to be.

The first principle is learning to learn. People learn when they are ready to learn and when what they are learning is interesting and engages their curiosity. Learning to learn requires an inquisitive mind which engages one in a process of self-discovery, of transcending the tyranny of one's own limited experience and being in a state of pushing forward and creating. This implies that the student is the initiator and prime mover in learning to learn and must accept responsibility for reaching out to new areas of discovery.

Learning to do gets at the relationship between achievement, productivity, industry, and the vitality of a free society. In the future, we must develop citizen-participants and citizen-producers rather than just citizen-consumers.

Learning to care touches some of the deepest human needs—the need to believe in something, to have faith, to belong, to feel wanted, to have an overarching, transcendent set of values which binds communities together. "Returning to basics" in education is not enough. Proficiency in arithmetic can be used to add up the day's take from illicit drugs. So arithmetic, speaking, writing, and other basic skills, alone, are not enough. A fundamentally humane purpose should inform and guide those skills.

Learning to be refers to finding that integrated, organic, wholeness of life. Being is an active verb and implies that competent, doing, caring people can make a difference. Learning to be is primarily an attitudinal objective and state of mind and can only be achieved by helping people gain perspective by discovering their very special place in a very special world.

This Declaration of Education is not a recipe book, but a set of principles. It suggests not so much what should be taught but more significantly the ends to which all learning should be devoted. This 1976 Declaration of Education fills that "emptiness at the core" of which some educational critics speak; it commits the Academy to preparing competent and concerned citizens, the kind of citizens which a free society deserves and demands.

("A 1976 Declaration of Education,"
Vital Speeches, January 15, 1977.)

The Risk of the Too-Narrow Mission

[In February 1978, Billy Wireman was elected President of Queens College, Charlotte, North Carolina, by the college's Board of Trustees. It was a gamble on both sides. In 1978, Queens suffered from a host of familiar but nevertheless potentially fatal maladies: tumbling enrollment, hemorrhaging finances, swelling debts, poor morale. The college's trustees gambled that the young president of Florida Presbyterian, now Eckerd College, could transform suffering Queens. And Billy Wireman gambled that he could organize a team that could not only save Queens but help it flourish. Queens's new president certainly brought a note of energy to the school; his passion for world travel was still powerful, and in the fall of 1978, he led a Charlotte delegation to China. His journalism bloomed, and he became a regular guest columnist for the Charlotte Observer. *Most importantly, he energized the Queens community and inaugurated a range of experiments designed to refloat, and then relaunch, the college. Queens, at that time still a women's college, continued to recruit traditional-aged women, but it also developed programs for adult students. Queens started an evening school serving especially working adults. It began a Master's of Business Administration program to serve Charlotte's fast-growing business community. The little school that had been politely dying sud-*

denly developed spunk. The focus on the part-time, working, adult learners was a particular passion of Dr. Wireman's. In this 1979 article, Dr. Wireman discusses the adult learner.]

J oining the traditional back-to-school student this fall will be an exploding student population in America, the adult learner, often called "the new majority," which includes approximately 65 million Americans. Roughly 15 million of these adult learners will be in traditional colleges and universities, leaving 50 million to be educated by other agencies in society, the military, corporations, labor unions, the government, and others. The sheer size, complexity, and guaranteed growth of this new adult market poses serious problems, but at the same time presents a host of exciting opportunities for the traditional educational establishment.

We might learn a lesson from the railroads, which shortsightedly defined their business as moving people and things by rail, as opposed to the much broader concept of transportation. Those schools and colleges which define their mission broadly and imaginatively to engage the adult learner can move to new levels of service and distinction. Those who define their mission too narrowly will fall by the wayside.

("THE ADULT LEARNER: EDUCATION'S
NEW CHALLENGE," *Miami Herald,*
SEPTEMBER 23, 1979.)

Why Queens College Is Important

*[On Queens's Founders Day, September 26, 1979, Queens's
new president argued that Queens had a bright future. In the
process, he defined qualities central to his vision of higher
education in America.]*

I want to suggest a number of specific reasons why
Queens College is important. The reasons are
grounded not so much in what is best for Queens,
but in what are the broader needs of human freedom in
our time.

• QUEENS IS PRIVATE. At a time when we are over-
whelmed by insensitive bureaucracies, huge deficits, infla-
tion, and inertia, Queens is under the control of a private
Board of Trustees, a group of volunteers who serve because they believe deeply in preserving and strengthening
the private sector of American life.

• QUEENS IS SMALL. When interlocking forces conspire
to dehumanize and fragment us, Queens is a community
where people know people, where problems can be talked
out, where lasting friendships can be made, where the
human dimension is paramount.

• QUEENS IS CHURCH-RELATED. At a time when we
have seemingly lost our roots, Queens stands

unapologetically in the great tradition of finding creative relationships between faith and reason. Force and strength without humane, moral, and spiritual direction are too terrible to contemplate. Queens calls us to the enduring, to the transcendent, to the "impenetrable mystery" in life.

• QUEENS IS DEVOTED TO THE LIBERAL ARTS. The liberal arts give meaning to an often meaningless world. Through them, we come to know who we are and where we have been. The liberal arts help us in the search for enlightenment and understanding. They help us to synthesize our experience and make our lives whole and rich.

• QUEENS IS DEVOTED TO THE NEW LEARNER. When an increasing number of Americans are struggling desperately to adapt and re-orient their lives in the midst of rapid change, Queens is reaching out in new and creative ways to the adult learner. These new learners enrich the total Queens academic community.

• QUEENS IS DEEPLY ROOTED IN "WHAT HAS BEEN." We have assessed, accurately, we hope, "what is." We have responded to this on the basis of "what is likely to be," and, I add, with a heavy dose of "what ought to be."

("FOUNDERS DAY REMARKS," SEPTEMBER 26, 1979.)

Focus on the Human Need

[Somehow, Queens's new president found time, between re-organizing programs and raising unprecedented amounts of money, to travel around the world. He traveled extensively in Asia and quickly became a key figure in the United Board for Christian Higher Education in Asia; as an educational consultant, he would travel to Brazil, to India, and to Africa. In part, to be sure, this simply represented Billy Wireman's exuberant energy and his passion for exploration. It also reflected his conviction that what would later be called "globalization" was well underway by the 1970s, and that anyone seriously interested in education for the 21st century had to adopt a global vision. As a consultant, Billy Wireman was a visionary, but he was also the practical expert, full of ideas about programs, management, fundraising, and organization. People around the world, with schools to reform, or with funds to raise, turned to Billy Wireman. Here is some practical advice, in a 1982 article, on fundraising.]

Never start negatively, with some problem. Instead, first focus on the human need to be met. We are not raising money, we are transforming human potentiality into human actuality. People do not give to gloom, doom, and despair. They give to promise, optimism, opportunity, enthusiasm, and causes which successfully fulfill human aspirations.

The cause, whatever it may be, must be competently managed and we must be effective stewards of donations. Studies have shown that too much money fails to get to the actual purpose of institutions raising those funds. We must always be prepared to answer the question: "What percentage of my gift will go to the people who are really in need?"

Never start with a rational explanation or justification of the cause. The head and the pocketbook are reached through the heart. People become engaged with issues first, and then they act on this engagement. The first step, then, is to engage people as powerfully as we can to the cause we wish to pursue.

("Vision, Competence, and Human Need," *The Crier*, October 1982.)

To Serve, Not Survive

[The day-to-day work of the college enterprise only makes sense within a morally specific context, as Billy Wireman constantly reminded his colleagues at Queens.]

Most colleges are asking the wrong question. They're asking, "how can we survive?" when they ought to be asking "how can we serve?"

("1981-82 President's Report," Queens College, 1982.)

The Higher Education Identity Crisis

[The eighties were a turbulent time in the world. They began with a re-heating of the Cold War, and ended with the collapse of the Berlin Wall, the Soviet Union, and Communism. In the summer of 1981, Dr. Wireman visited Brazil at the invitation of President Edmund Meuwissen of the Benevolentia Foundation to critique Catholic higher education in that country. As with many church-related institutions of higher learning, financial matters were the most pressing issues for the Catholic colleges Dr. Wireman visited. Dr. Wireman applied his keen business sense to the colleges' situations. There, as in the U.S., Wireman saw institutions focusing too much on immediate problems and not enough on a strategic vision and mission to attract long-term support among influential people and in the community as a whole. Institutions of higher learning, he argued throughout his career, must know what they are about, must respond to the needs of society, and must articulate their value to those they serve and from whom they seek support.]

The rectors are spending too much time on immediate problems. This is understandable, but the consequence is that a serious and sustained effort to create futures for the universities is, by and large, being neglected. The universities are in an identity crisis. In Brazil and indeed throughout the world, higher education needs to do a better job of convincing a skeptical public of its importance. No longer can we assume that the university has an inherent right to exist.

No more important or pressing challenge faces the universities than to construct a clear, Christian, explicit, strong, compelling, distinctive, Brazilian-rooted case for the Catholic university in Brazil. This exciting vision must then be shared with those who can help to achieve it. Nothing serious can be done about longterm viability until this step is taken.

There is not a clear-cut understanding of, or agreement on, whether the future of the Catholic university is principally with the Church and the private sector or with the government. It is not a question of either/or, but rather one of relative dominance and focus. Institutions, like individuals, must have motivational roots, forces which energize their behavior and provide inspiration for the struggle which accompanies any worthwhile cause. In the private, Christian sector, these forces and roots must be transcendent in nature and further must be grounded in meeting human needs and human hopes with options that are indigenous to the country's, the Church's, the human family's highest and most noble aspirations. The focus must be on meaning and ultimate worth, on transforming human knowledge into human wisdom within a perspective of time and eternity. Edmund Meuwissen's concern for values, which I share, can best be expressed by searching for creative links between faith and reason.

Institutions, in short, should know who they are, who they are *not*, what they stand for, the distinctiveness they embody, and what would be lost and to whom if they did not exist. Catholic universities in Brazil, like church-related universities in America and throughout the world, need to do a lot of work on these questions. Never in human history have we so desperately needed trained and disciplined intelligence, guided by humane and moral purpose. What a need! What an opportunity!

("CATHOLIC HIGHER EDUCATION IN
BRAZIL: A FUTURE TO CHOOSE OR
LOSE," *Report to the Benevolentia
Foundation*, JUNE 5, 1981.)

BEGIN WITH THE VISION

[Two things appear abundantly clear in Dr. Wireman's approach to higher education: an academic institution must be prepared to change to meet the needs of the community it serves, and it must have a clearly articulated educational goal to which the community can respond with enrollments and financial support. The second point lies at the heart of Dr. Wireman's genius as a fundraiser.]

Effective fundraising is having a good cause and asking others to join in helping it succeed. Again, I emphasize the cause must be grounded in meeting a human, spiritual, cultural, academic, or other worthwhile need. Approaching fundraising on the above principles will ensure that the cause endures. The wisdom is as simple and old as the ancient scriptures: "Where there is no vision, the people perish."

Let's begin with the vision and then proceed to ask others to help us achieve it. So simple, yet so true.

("VISION, COMPETENCE, HUMAN NEED:
KEYS TO EFFECTIVE FUNDRAISING,"
[CHARLOTTE] *Crier*, DECEMBER, 1982.)

On Reason, Wisdom, Justice, and Love

[At Queens College, Dr. Wireman began early in his presidency to articulate the unique purpose and mission of the private liberal arts college and his definition of the goals of education. He frequently explored this issue in his remarks to the faculty of Queens College at the opening of the school year, as he does in this 1983 address, later reprinted in the school newspaper.]

I t is with a deep sense of joy and anticipation that I welcome you to the Queens community for the school year '83-'84. There is always something exciting about a beginning. Old faces greet the new; fresh relationships are formed; slowly a community comes into being; summer memories fade into fall studies; and a refreshingly cool nip hangs beseechingly in the night air. A certain rhythm settles in.

In the hustle and bustle of it all, let us not forget what it is we are about. Queens is a learning community. Education at its deepest levels is a search for enlightenment, understanding, and meaning. Search is an active verb and implies struggle and the unknown. The more we learn the more we find there is to learn—so we bring a certain humility to our academic and intellectual pursuits.

There is joy and mystery, awe and wonder, spontaneity, and a certain amount of just plain hard work and persistence inherent in a serious academic community.

Queens is also a church-related college. This gives us a special distinction.

There is an Impenetrable Mystery to life. Plumb the depths of the human spirit and we encounter our destiny. Let us individually and collectively search for that creative juxtaposition between faith and reason, between the life of the mind and the life of the spirit. We are a community engaged in a common struggle—seeking new relationships, new insights, finding new connections, integrating what we learn into what we already know—in short, attempting to bring wholeness out of fragmentation and specialization. Let's make '83-'84 the year we transform human hopes and human dreams into human wisdom and human achievement. Let's do this through the hallmarks of the serious church-related college: reason and wisdom and justice and love.

In that spirit, and with the fond hope that this will be your best year ever, I welcome each of you. This is your place and your time on earth. Let's rejoice together in the many opportunities which are ours.

("Dr. Billy O. Wireman," *Queens Current*, August 19, 1983.)

Avoiding the New Illiteracy

[What is a university like? To what can we compare it? Some would argue that a university is like a corporation. Billy Wireman would certainly agree that a university must be efficient, sensitive to its market, and financially sound. Yet for Billy Wireman, a university is much more like a church than a corporation. The whole point of the university is to serve the community, the nation, the world, the future, and, above all, the students. Stewardship, not ownership, and service, not self-interest, are central to the spiritual core Dr. Wireman thought should energize the university. How appropriate, then, that Queens College's motto is "not to be served, but to serve." This stress on service and stewardship recurs throughout Dr. Wireman's thinking about education, for instance, in this 1986 interview with the Charlotte Observer.*]*

We must position a college to meet the needs of the community. You don't ask, "How can I save myself?" You ask, "How can I meet the needs of others?" It's almost the old Christian principle that to save your life, you lose it in service. So if you ask the larger questions—what are the deficiencies in society and how can I respond?—the answers afford us some exciting opportunities. It seems to me that we have in our society a shoddiness, a lack of concern for quality that is far too pervasive. Any institution of higher learning worth its salt has to see its mission as developing competent human beings. There is a great opportunity in our society to do a good job with that.

There is also the issue of what I call cognitive and conceptual unity. By that, I mean that our lives become so fragmented in this era of specialization that we are losing our ability to see the whole, even our interest in seeing the whole. It is a new form of illiteracy. We are drifting through life without knowing what is taking place.

And a third area that I see as very important is developing a moral sensitivity—a willingness and ability to ask the larger ethical questions.

I can't imagine a greater need than confronting those challenges, and a liberal arts institution is uniquely positioned to help us look at that future. It is an exciting challenge and opportunity for the academy.

("Queens Today: Wireman Sees New Opportunities to Serve," Interview with Frye Gaillard in the *Charlotte Observer*, September, 1986.)

To Manage Change Proactively

[The ability to change to meet the needs of a society is also of paramount importance in Dr. Wireman's concept of what makes an academic institution vital and necessary and worthy of support. In the late 1980s, Queens College went through a series of changes to revitalize its mission and attract more local support by providing new programs for the Charlotte community. In 1987, the college decided to admit males after more than a hundred years as a woman's college. An internship became part of the basic undergraduate curriculum; an international component was added, too; and all students were required to complete an interdisciplinary, team-taught, core curriculum in the liberal arts. All this was a tremendous change for the college. In fact, in Dr. Wireman's mind, change is precisely one of those things for which the academy is intended to prepare its students. This is the point Dr. Wireman argues in this 1990 talk to students.]

The best preparation for your future is to learn to respond coherently and creatively to life's only constant: unpredictable and unplanned change. The required four-year, seven-course Foundations in Liberal Learning sequence will help you cope with this hard reality.

By examining critically history's triumphs and tragedies, your decisions will be better informed. In the process, you will come to understand your heritage and also establish a moral vision for your future. Further, the small-seminar format of liberal learning forces intensive interdisciplinary concentration on the basic skills of reading, writing, speaking, listening, conceptualizing, and finding connections. Combine these skills with requirements in science, math and language, your international experience and community internship, and you have a first-rate liberal education—the best guarantee for a life of curiosity, discovery, and renewal.

Seven events which have occurred since you were about to enter high school in 1986—each with its own message—dramatize the necessity to prepare for unrelenting change.

On January 28, 1986, the American spaceship Challenger disintegrated 74 seconds after launch, killing all seven astronauts.

Message: There is no technological certainty. All humanly devised systems are subject to error.

On April 28, 1986, in the Ukrainian town of Chernobyl, a Soviet nuclear reactor malfunctioned, resulting in a meltdown. Poisonous radioactive material drifted into Scandinavia and Europe.

Message: No country lives in isolation from its neighbors. It is one planet with one fragile environment. Our lives are inextricably intertwined. We are indeed "our brother's keeper."

On May 29, 1987, 21-year-old West German Mathias Rust flew from Helsinki, Finland, in a small, rented private plane and landed in Moscow's Red Square, startling and embarrassing Soviet officialdom. Rust penetrated the most expensive and elaborate air defense system in history.

Message: There is no security in military defense. Human will and ingenuity will win out in the end.

On October 16, 1987, the Dow Jones Index fell 500 points, the largest one-day drop in history. Unanticipated, this sharp decline unsettled the world's economic and political structures.

Message: Life is interdisciplinary. The world is all connected. When abrupt change occurs, when some far-distant bell tolls, it may be that it, as John Donne writes, "tolls for thee."

On November 9, 1989, the Berlin Wall crumbled. Germany would be reunited and Eastern Europe would be free of forty years of Soviet bondage. Wild jubilation erupted on both sides of the Wall. Overnight, the Cold

War became a Street Dance.

Message: The human spirit is indomitable. Artificial walls cannot squelch people's desire for freedom.

On February 11, 1990, South African President F. W. de Klerk released Nelson Mandela after 27 years of imprisonment. Mandela's stoic, charitable attitude won the world. One of his first requests after release was, "Let's not do anything which would lead anyone to question our capacity to govern ourselves."

Message: Quiet dignity and moral conviction are still powerful examples. Courage—"grace under pressure," in Hemingway's catching phrase—is stronger than prison walls.

On August 2, 1990, after repeated assurances to the contrary, Iraqi President Saddam Hussein invaded Kuwait. The result was the largest American military build-up since Vietnam and a dangerously inflamed world situation.

Message: The international Cold War may have ended, but regional Hot Wars have not. Regional conflicts driven by religion, race and tribe are more difficult to settle than big-power conflicts, which are typically motivated by political ideology. Your world will be multi-polar, which is more dangerous than a bi-polar one. America dares not reduce its military below levels capable of preserving order. The world is still, in John F. Kennedy's words, "an untidy place." Public television's Bill Moyers calls it "the search for values, faith and meaning." Historian Arthur Schlesinger, Jr., describes it as "the long, stumbling march toward human freedom." Name it what you will, it's the issue of our time: the struggle by people to be governed by what Alexander Hamilton called "freedom and choice" rather than "accident and force."

By equipping you with a conscientious and morally sensitive intellect, liberal education teaches you to manage change proactively and thus be a constructive participant in that struggle. Government by freedom and choice requires this kind of education.

("COHERENCE THROUGH LIBERAL EDUCATION, BEST PREPARATION FOR CHANGE," *Charlotte Observer*, SEPTEMBER 24, 1990.)

The Case for Multicultural Education

[By the 1990s, Dr. Wireman had become a tireless advocate for multicultural and international education. Here is just one of many pleas he made to the academy to open its doors and its minds to the wider world.]

The academy's main purpose is to prepare competent citizens to cope with a rapidly changing world. To be sure, that process begins at home. Westerners cannot know themselves well unless they know the Bible, the Greeks, and the Romans. But those insights must be connected to current reality. That's how learning occurs.

Today's students live in a different world. In the 50 years prior to 1965, 75 percent of the 11 million American immigrants were of European ancestry. In the last quarter-century, of 14 million U.S. immigrants, only 15 percent were of European origin. Women now constitute more than 50 percent of the American workforce. Extrapolate those trends over the next 50 years and the shape of 21st century America emerges.

We are now in a conflict with Islamic fundamentalism, which few understand. With the disintegration of the Soviet Union, America is the last superpower, the one nation which combines political, economic and military strength able to shape world events.

With the military conflict in the Persian Gulf over, America must lead in the painful process of building a lasting peace. That will require unprecedented levels of international cooperation and understanding, which can be achieved only through multicultural education.

("COLLEGES MUST OFFER MULTICULTURAL EDUCATION," *Charlotte Observer*, MARCH 16, 1991.)

The Key to Democratic Prosperity

[In the 1990s, Dr. Wireman's predictions about the importance of international awareness to education came true. "Globalization" convinced even the most rigid isolationists that education, particularly liberal arts education, had to be global. This is a point Dr. Wireman made in this 1994 article.]

F ounded by Sir Walter Raleigh in 1585 as a trading post, North Carolina now faces its greatest business challenge: to compete successfully in today's global village. Even though North Carolina in 1993 was the nation's 12th-largest exporter of manufactured goods—$8.6 billion—this is no time to gloat.

Global competition requires that we strengthen international education for business leadership. Why is this important? The numbers tell the story:

- In July, Charlotte became the nation's fastest growing city for exports—totaling $1.8 billion in 1993—up 254 percent from 1987. That's better than Atlanta, New York, or Los Angeles. Also in July, Charlotte was chosen as a trade promotion office by the Clinton administration.

- In Charlotte, the number of foreign-owned firms rose from 75 in 1990 to 118 in 1993. That number in 1960: 18.
- Within the 13-county Metro Charlotte Region, there are 442 foreign firms.
- The Vietnam embargo is gone: 70 million people—more than England or France—need "everything."
- NAFTA—the North American Free Trade Agreement—will open Mexico's 90 million people to American business.

From Beijing to Budapest, from Mexico City to Madagascar, the story is the same: People want better lives for themselves. And they want them now. Where better to prepare North Carolina business leadership for this challenge than in our colleges and universities?

That's why, in 1986, then Queens College Chairman Bill Lee of Duke Power appointed a task force to formulate a future for Queens. Task force member and NationsBank Chairman Hugh McColl, Jr., Queens's chairman (and for whom Queens's School of Business is named), cut quickly to the point: "What is our market niche? Why should business support Queens? How are we distinctive?"

Today, we need only point to Queens's "products" to

answer Hugh McColl's questions and to see why Spelman College President Johnnetta Cole told Queens's 1994 graduates, "You have had one of the most unique combinations of learning experiences in America." Consider:

- Kentuckian Kathryn Stanley, 21, a senior business major in the McColl School, spent six weeks last summer as one of two American students who interned with *The Wall Street Journal Europe* in Brussels. Three other Queens students interned with firms in Paris, Madrid, and Vienna. They were part of the McColl School European Internship Program, made possible by a group of Charlotte business leaders headed by Philipp Holzmann President Dieter Rathke.
- McColl School Executive MBA student Anna Walsh, 26, of Charlotte, has studied with Queens in Brazil, Chile and Asia. Walsh, a UNC-Chapel Hill graduate, said that "travel has opened my eyes to many international opportunities. Queens is very farsighted to make these trips available to all students."
- Bob Denault, 36, a 1993 McColl School Executive MBA graduate, was recently assigned to Indonesia by his company, Asea Brown Boveri Combustion Engineering Services. He visited Asia in 1992 with a Queens study tour.

The country or culture or corporation or college that

discovers the key to galvanizing democracy, the market, and cultural pluralism into engines which produce a prosperous democracy and a democratic prosperity will lead the world.

Why shouldn't North Carolina be among those leaders?

("SURVIVING IN THE GLOBAL VILLAGE: NORTH CAROLINA'S FUTURE DEPENDS ON INTERNATIONAL EDUCATION," *North Carolina*, SEPTEMBER, 1994.)

America's Third Frontier

[At the heart of Dr. Wireman's philosophy of education is an immersion in the liberal arts which he defines as "an encounter with ideas that help us develop morally sensitive intellects, a process which converts human knowledge into human wisdom, reshaped to human hope and human fulfillment." After visiting a Charlotte high school class in American history, Dr. Wireman mused on the role public education plays in building a better society. America, he notes, began as a "new frontier," a frontier that we are still exploring and building through the education of our young people.]

Searching for better lives, 60 million pioneers immigrated through America's first frontier—the Eastern seaboard. Slowly, we settled the West, America's second frontier. Now we face a third, non-geographical frontier, at once future-oriented and morally based, continuing to correct the legacy of slavery, expanding opportunities for women, and mastering the information revolution. Additionally, we must heal the ugly wounds symbolized by Waco and Oklahoma City, and adjust to a new ethnically explosive world struggling between globalism and tribalism. And the current efforts to right America's economic house must succeed.

American youth too often get a bad rap. While some do go wrong, the high school students I met with, like millions of young Americans of all ages and races, want to be conscientious citizens. They care about their families, their schools, their churches. But they are troubled about America's future.

To perpetuate America as a frontier, we must work with the young to create an enlightened and just society, one that is fiscally sound and built on incentive, opportunity and merit, and undergirded by moral values.

("Renewing American Civilization,"
Charlotte Observer, June 13, 1995.)

Productive Careers and Noble Lives

[In 1996, Dr. Wireman was invited to be the keynote speaker at Han Nam University's fortieth anniversary celebrations. In Taejon, South Korea, at Han Nam, Dr. Wireman made the following remarks. They are printed here at some length because they summarize so much of his thinking about education.]

During the past forty years, as you have worked to create this fine Presbyterian institution, I too have worked, on the other side of the world, with your sister Presbyterian colleges.

Only four years after Han Nam was founded in 1956, I joined the faculty of the brand new Florida Presbyterian College, now Eckerd College, in St. Petersburg, Florida. I served there as professor, dean, vice-president, and, from 1968-1977, as president. Early in 1978, I assumed the presidency of Queens College.

The forty years since 1956 have been among the most tumultuous in human history. We have experienced the end of the Industrial Era and the beginning of the Information Age. After spending trillions of dollars on military defense, we have watched Communism collapse under its own weight. We all witnessed the symbolic end of the twentieth century on November 9, 1989, when the Berlin Wall fell and the Cold War turned into a street dance overnight.

Quickly, however, that euphoric moment was vaporized by harsh realities and we moved from "poetic promise to accounting." Indeed, we now are challenged to do the "rough work of freedom," to ensure, as former U.S. President George H. W. Bush says, that "freedom's time does not turn into a nightmare."

Last fall, after speaking at Soong Sil University in Seoul, I boarded a plane and flew directly to Beijing. I marveled that such a flight, all but impossible and unthinkable only a few years ago, has become a routine occurrence.

In America, the last forty years have been exceedingly turbulent: the heroic Civil Rights and Women's movements, the tragic war in Vietnam, the violent deaths of John Kennedy, Robert Kennedy, Martin Luther King, and Malcolm X, the political turmoil surrounding Presidents Johnson and Nixon, the dramatic transformation of our economy—all of these events punctuated a tumultuous time.

Since 1960, American higher education has experienced explosive growth. From three million students in 1960, America now has nearly 15 million college students. We have done a splendid job in opening access to higher education. But now we must turn to the focus, quality, and substance of what students are learning. Here, we have some work to do.

In Korea, as in America, the last four decades have been dramatic. You have recovered from a devastating war. You have created and preserved democracy, in spite of storms of controversies and dangers. You have become masters of commerce and an economic model to the world. You have been faithful stewards of the church—as I'm sure you know, there are more Presbyterians in Korea than in America; perhaps it's time you sent missionaries to us.

This is my twenty-fifth trip to Asia. Each time I come I see more evidence of the "Asian economic miracle." And for me, coming to Han Nam University is like coming home. Your generous hospitality and your beautiful campus evoke fond and rich memories in my spirit.

Two concepts are keys to our future, I think: productive careers and noble lives. We must design academic programs and institutions which unite these two powerful ideas and use them to transform our students' lives. Either concept alone is an orphan. Together, the two can become a forceful theme for liberal education in the twenty-first century.

First, let me describe where I think we are today. Second, let me suggest where we should be going. Third, let me explain concretely what I mean by productive careers and noble lives.

Let's define where we are today.

Our time is marked, above all, by the universal failure of ideology. With this collapse of ideology has come the opportunity for a sustained, world-wide economic expansion, a development that could raise the living standards of millions of now impoverished people throughout the world. Managing this economic explosion will require morally based leadership skills unprecedented in human history. And where will these leaders' values be shaped? Where better than in the world's colleges and universities, especially those related to the church?

Around the world, ideology is dead or dying. Now, by the demise of ideology I do not mean the demise of ideas. Quite the contrary. Ideas have never been more important. But ideas now must be connected to harnessing this vast engine of growth and development.

By ideology, I mean those closed, rigid, and dogmatic fantasies of secular utopias which festered through the twentieth century. Ideology haunted our planet for much of the twentieth century: fascism, communism, racism, imperialism, and militaristic nationalism enslaved the bodies and minds of millions. Hatreds fueled by ideology left much of the world in blood and ashes.

But, at least for now, ideology is waning. Fascism as an organized system is dead; communism as a viable social system is dying. I remember visiting the office of now Czech President Vaclav Havel in Prague in 1990, and seeing a sign which read: "We want Democracy, Market Economics, and Pluralism." For millions throughout the world, this will be the motto of the next century.

Democracy, the free market, and cultural and political pluralism are the very opposite of ideology. They represent individual freedom, choice, diversity, and mobility. Democracy, the free market, and pluralism are all rooted in an intense respect for people, a commitment to popular sovereignty and to the rule of law. And around the world, this is what is in people's hearts.

Visit any area in the world—Asia, America, Russia, Latin America, Africa—and you see bright, young women and men entrepreneurs, cellular phones in hand, working on some project.

Their task is to make things work. We have moved from utopian, wild speculation to cautious planning, from fanaticism to prudence, from fantasy to the burdens and joys of daily life. It is this idea of making things better that challenges us now. Around the world, the great task before us is creating goods and services and living the responsible and rewarding life. We have moved from words to work. Creating the conditions of a decent life is no small task, particularly in a world in which poverty, and even famine, is a daily reality for millions.

Economics has become for the moment the new master science. In America, on almost every college campus, more and more students are studying business and economics. And I find that students, no matter what academic discipline they study, are concerned, above all, with preparing themselves for the world of work.

Connecting productive careers with the life of the mind and good citizenship is a dignified and even heroic act. It encourages modesty, care, and values. Why? Because each generation must remember that it is heir to a great legacy. Many of our forebearers cared deeply about civic and political integrity. As Scripture tells us: "We live in cities we did not build." One of the duties of each generation is to pass on to its children cities and a world that are safer, cleaner, and healthier.

To create nourishing foods, safer streets, potent medicines, better houses, great cities, stimulating schools, jobs and opportunities for the young, and safety and security for the old, are tasks of great importance. And Asia has shown the world the way. In the last forty years, in Asia, nearly two billion people have risen from poverty; terrible illnesses have receded; minds crippled by illiteracy and ignorance have been cured by education. The achievements of Korea in particular fill the rest of the world with awe.

But yet, even as our young people are learning marketable skills, I sense an uneasiness about them and their lives. While denouncing the failed ideologies of the past, they search at the same time for meaning which will enrich and enhance their lives.

Like you, I work with young people every day, and I am struck by their genuine hunger for meaning. They realize that democracy and markets and pluralism without moral vision are hollow shells. They are not cynics; nor are they materialists. Instead, they yearn for truth, and direction, and purpose. And they realize, like Dostoyevsky, that "without God, any horror is possible."

And here, a profound change in thinking is needed. What people in general, and young people in particular, yearn for is not therapy.

What they really yearn for is wisdom. We need a great revival of the wisdom traditions of the world. We need institutions which speak to life and its purposes, death and its meaning, work and its values. As believers, especially, we need to remember that what we preach is not simply dry abstract assertions, and that what we offer is not simply another form of social organization. Rather, we should try to practice what we preach.

If what I have said is true, what, then, are we as scholars at church-related colleges to do? I believe that we ought to create an education that will lead to productive careers and noble lives.

We have to ensure that the ballot and market are stamped by humane values.

Let us recall that the liberal arts, those abilities to speak and act thoughtfully and coherently, first evolved, in ancient times, not as academic specialties but as the practical tools of the citizen. The liberal arts were designed not as aids in speculation, but as means for action. Thus, we must recognize that helping students achieve productive and noble lives has become again a central theme of the liberal arts.

Is it wrong for students to wish to learn to work productively and well, with skill and dignity? I think not. Rather, to be concerned with work, with craft, with competence, is something to applaud. Vaclav Havel often condemned Communist regimes for their disdain for the realities of people's daily lives. To return to reality from propaganda and lies is a step toward recovering humanity.

Scholars should have no fear of the world of work. To the contrary, who better could help guide students in the ways of this world? Scholarly theory, research, and speculation will continue to be essential to the life of the mind. But this connection must have roots; it *must* be accountable to today, and it must have a home in a creative interaction between thought and action, between work and citizenship. Havel again gives us insight:

> The only real hope of people today is a renewal of the certainty that we are rooted in the Earth and, at the same time, the cosmos. This awareness endows us with the capacity for self-transcendence. Politicians at international forums may reiterate a thousand times that the basis of the new world order must be universal respect

for human rights, but it will mean nothing as long as this imperative does not derive from the respect of the miracle of being, the miracle of the universe, the miracle of nature, the miracle of our own existence.

As scholars and intellectuals, we should have no fear of finding connections between the life of the mind, these impenetrable miracles, and the marketplace.

But there is another task as well.

I mentioned before that our young people have a genuine hunger and thirst for wisdom. From history, they are acutely aware that force and strength without humane direction are too terrible to contemplate. We need but to look at Hitler or the savagery in Cambodia and parts of Africa to be reminded that productive careers must be wedded to noble lives. In my country, we have work to do in lowering crime rates and drug abuse. Recent ethnic cleansing episodes are painful reminders of how far we have to go. And students will turn for counsel to those of us who are committed to finding connections and relevancy between intellectual inquiry and the correction of these social injustices.

When I speak of noble lives I mean three things: character, conscience, and community.

By character, I mean those personal qualities or virtues which mold us as human beings. I have yet to find a society in which cowardice was praised over courage, selfishness was prized instead of generosity, or ignorance was preferred to wisdom. Expressions of courage, generosity, and wisdom take many and differing forms; customs and cultures are very different. But, as human beings, we ought to praise courage and generosity and wisdom whether we find them in America, or Korea, or Africa, or anywhere, and we ought to repudiate cowardice, selfishness, and ignorance wherever they are found.

Character needs to be grown and nurtured. It needs to be strengthened daily. We need to recover the world's great wisdom traditions, the world's ancient schools of virtue. We can still learn from Aristotle and Confucius and the other ancient sages. But we must too return to the virtues of justice and mercy embedded in our Judeo-Christian heritage.

Noble lives also mean conscience, that spark of Divinity within each of us which we recognize as the Spirit who prompts and corrects us always. It is an old and hallowed tradition that calls us, above all other things, to be true to our conscience. To act against our conscience is always illicit. But we also must work to have an informed and correct conscience. We must be sure that we do not mistake our own voice, or some other human voice, for the voice of the Spirit. We must learn to discern the voice of the Spirit within us, and where better can one learn to discern the Spirit than in academies founded by the church?

Noble lives also include a deep concern for Community. Character and conscience flourish only in communities which value them. To be a member of a community is to be a citizen, a participant in the life, and suffering, and triumphs of the community. Indeed, without a civil society, character and conscience wither.

The heroes of our time, from Vaclav Havel to Nelson Mandela, have called on us to rebuild and restore communities of harmony and trust so that character and conscience may flourish. When Nelson Mandela was released from prison, for example, he was asked whether he intended to take revenge on his persecutors. Mandela responded that he had no time for revenge because he would be too busy rebuilding his nation. Francis Fukuyama has written that mutual trust is the essential social capital without which nations perish. To be an active and vigorous citizen within a community which honors character and conscience is central to living a noble life.

As I reflect on the work that both Queens and Han Nam have done, I believe that we are both moving ahead and coming home. We are going ahead into the 21st century, developing an education for students yet unborn. Each season has its unique dangers and opportunities; what worked a generation ago may not work well for the next. We must be able to change, adapt, reform, and re-create.

And yet, it seems that as we move forward, we are also

moving deeper and deeper into our heritage. We are becoming more and more who we should be by returning to the ancient calling of scholars and recognizing work as worthy of respect.

In 2036, Han Nam University will celebrate its 80th birthday. Another celebration will no doubt be held here on this beautiful campus on a crisp fall day.

The audience that day will represent a prosperous, united, democratic Korea, in an Asia on the move. China will be a world superpower. And the speakers will be asked to reflect on the 80-year history of Han Nam University, especially our stewardship of the last 40 years. And I wonder what our heirs will say of us?

I hope that they will say that we responded to the challenges of our time with care and humility.

I hope they will realize that, even as we constructed new and innovative educational programs for them, we preserved the intimate relationship between reason and faith which is the heart of our kind of education.

I hope that they will say that we continued the ancient work of spreading wisdom throughout the world by both precept and example.

I hope our heirs honestly can say that we were good stewards and that we left the world better than we found it.

I hope they will say that we worked diligently to find new insights into the critical relation between productive, rewarding work and responsible citizenship expressed in a noble life.

I hope they say that we shaped the 21st century economic expansion to moral ends, and that we remembered the scriptural injunction: "If you have done it to the least of these, you have done it to me."

If our successors can honestly say these things, then we will be worthy of the ultimate scriptural tributes:

"You fought the good fight . . . you kept the faith." "Well done, thy good and faithful servants."

("Productive Careers & Noble Lives: A New Mandate for a Liberal Arts Education," *Address Delivered to Han Nam University on its 40th Anniversary Celebration,* Traejon, South Korea, October 17, 1996.)

Presidential Effectiveness

[By the late 1990s, Dr. Wireman had become something of an expert on being a college president. In this little speech, he offers advice (and sympathy) to current and future presidents.]

This is a conversation between a mother and her son or daughter.

Mother: "It's time to get up and go to school! Hurry or you'll be late!"

Child: "I'm not going to school today!"

Mother: "You've got to go! Now get a move on!"

Child: "I hate school! I'm not going!"

Mother: "I'm ashamed of you! Tell me why you hate school."

Child: "The food's no good. The faculty are arrogant. The students are surly. It's a miserable place. Give me two good reasons why I should go!"

Mother: "First, you're forty-two years old. Second, you're the president!"

For present and future college presidents, I offer the following fifteen steps as a guide to presidential effectiveness—and sanity!

- Have a strategic vision and state it often.
- Respect and emphasize the "life of the mind."
- Write your own speeches.
- Confirm the centrality of the faculty.
- Speak and write often about social justice.
- Read the student newspaper.
- Develop a head for numbers.
- Know when to talk, when to listen, and when to decide—and then decide!
- Get to know, and like, and genuinely be interested in the students.
- Be kind to your predecessors.
- Visit all your friends, the Board of Trustees, the Alums, Parents, Donors, Foundations, and so on, on *their* turf.
- Maintain an intellectual, spiritual, and personal life independent of your work.
- Understand, and practice, MBWA—"management by walking around."
- Take your work, *not yourself,* seriously.
- Know when to hold 'em, know when to fold 'em, know when to walk away, know when to run.

(SACS ANNUAL MEETING, SESSION FOR NEW PRESIDENTS, 1999 AND 2000.)

BECOMING CHANGE AGENTS

[As he began his third decade in higher education in the 1990s, Dr. Wireman focused increasingly on the need to prepare students for the inevitability of change. To endure and above all to master change, students have to be skilled, quick, but intensely spiritual. Without that spiritual grounding, mastery has no direction, and endurance no purpose. To endure and above all master change, to become, in the language of the 1990s, an "agent of change," is the subject of this 1998 speech.]

I am here today to talk about a force that affects us all, the force of change. We can approach this powerful force in two different ways. We can passively submit to change, or we can become agents of change ourselves. As historian Will Durant puts it, controlling change "depends upon the presence or absence of initiative and of creative individuals with clarity of mind and energy of will capable of effective responses to new situations."

Today, I would like to build on Durant's statement and identify five characteristics of people who have made change happen in history, with the hopes that all of us here will be able to leave this room well-prepared to make a difference. In fact, current events make this topic all the more relevant.

The first characteristic of change agents that I would like to talk about is CREATIVITY. If we always approach situations in the same way, we will never have the option of wondering what it might be like in other circumstances. In fact, if we never employ creativity, we may never see a need or an opportunity at all. Creativity is akin to vision because creativity pushes us to think in terms of the future.

The second characteristic of a change agent is COURAGE. Courage to recognize what has been done in the past and then respectfully differ. Why do we always flip to the comics or to the sports page? Because, well, that's the way we've always done it. Habit is a powerful thing, and we are creatures of habit, but habit can be constrictive. I am not advocating change for change's sake, but I am advocating courageous change in situations where new methodology can be beneficial.

The third characteristic of a change agent is VISIBILITY. While one person's ideas and actions are extremely important, a change agent must have support for his/her cause. Of course, getting support entails being visible and letting people know that you are there and that you have an idea. Remember, out of sight means out of mind, and action speaks louder than words.

The fourth characteristic of a change agent is PERSE-VERANCE. Patience and sheer doggedness are required for any project to succeed. Obviously, if we stop short of our goal, nothing is achieved and our credibility is negatively impacted. Our stubbornness to stick with an idea shows that we are putting our money where our mouth is and it gets the job done.

Finally, the fifth and last characteristic that I would like to talk about today is DRIVING MOTIVATION. True change agents never step back and admire what they have done. They are too busy, pushing ahead to the next opportunity, to rest on their laurels. Change agents never die, they simply relocate.

("CHARACTERISTICS OF CHANGE
AGENTS: FIVE MODELS OF EFFECTIVE-
NESS," A SPEECH TO THE STRATEGIC
SOURCING GROUP OF FIRST UNION
CORPORATION, CHARLOTTE, NORTH
CAROLINA, OCTOBER 22, 1998.)

What Is a University For?

[Old questions never die, and they rarely fade away. In the 1960s, Billy Wireman began asking fundamental questions about the means and ends of higher education in America. In the 1990s, he was still pressing those questions. "What is a university for? What is its contribution to society? What would be lost if a university were to disappear from its immediate community?" An institution of higher learning, in Dr. Wireman's mind, must have a clearly delineated purpose and that purpose must be one of service to its community. "Sadly," he observes, "there is no coherent vision driving American higher education. Indeed, we are not even asking the basic educational questions: What should be taught? To whom? To what end?"]

Immediately after accepting the presidency of Florida Presbyterian College (now Eckerd) on May 3, 1968, I received a petition from campus radicals representing Students for a Democratic Society: "We will not be dehumanized. Dismantle the military, industrial complex." Thus I began my 30 years as a college president.

In 1968, four million American college students were equally split between public and private institutions. Virtually all were 18- to 22-year-olds. The American Council on Education found that "developing a meaningful philosophy of life" was college freshmen's top priority. "Becoming financially secure" was near last.

Martin Luther King had been assassinated a month earlier. Vietnam was ravaging the country, and the women's movement was exploding. Two black American gold medalists raised the "clenched fist" Black Power salute at the Mexico City Olympics; black radical Eldridge Cleaver's *Soul On Ice* outraged the establishment.

Bob Dylan's "Ballad of a Thin Man" captured America's mood: "You know something is happening, but you don't quite know what it is, do you, Mr. Jones?" An adviser to President Nixon thought he knew: "Godless communism is the enemy; 'hippy' campuses are seething in revolt; the 'Moral Majority' must save us."

In early 1969, I was invited to a White House education briefing. Nixon counselor George Schultz began by asking, *"What* is a university for? Does anyone know?"

A stony silence followed. Fast-forward to 1998, my 21st year as president of Queens College, after nine at Eckerd.

The unchanging question today was raised by Michael Hooker, chancellor of the University of North Carolina. Last December, he rephrased what Schultz said in 1969: "We know the value of a baccalaureate degree, but what does it certify?"

Same question, except the milieu for higher education and America has changed dramatically.

- Today, 15 million students attend college—80 percent in public institutions, 20 percent in private. Fifty percent are over 25. Women are a majority. Students are decidedly career-oriented.
- The "M and M" twins—meaning and money—have reversed. "Becoming financially secure" is the primary objective of college freshmen; "developing a meaningful philosophy of life" is near last.
- "Godless communism" is dead, evangelical Christianity is spreading rapidly, and the "Moral Majority" remains elusive.
- The new enemy is Saddam Hussein and our moral dilemmas are cloning and Internet pornography.
- An increase in the black middle-income population and access to higher education have given young blacks hope that America's promise is also theirs. Eldridge Cleaver is a "born again" Christian.

Higher education enrollment has quintupled, and millions of Americans—both young and old—have enriched their lives and improved their earning power. American higher education is the world's best. But, preoccupied with growth, we have given precious little thought to what students learn.

Sadly, there is no coherent vision driving American higher education. Indeed, we are not even asking the basic educational questions: What should be taught? To whom? To what end?

As the late Fred Hechinger, long-time education writer for *The New York Times*, observed: "There is at the heart of the university a collective vacuum begging to be filled with a vision of its own end."

Too often, scientists talk to scientists, historians talk to historians, artists talk to artists, and philosophers talk to God. Life is interdisciplinary, but the university remains compartmentalized. Students are the losers, when helping them learn to solve problems by developing synergism between learning and life should be our chief mission. A *Doonesbury* cartoon is insightful: A smiling college president, reflecting on a favorable balance sheet, asks, "I wonder if anyone is learning anything?"

Astonishingly, a student can, through careful selection, graduate from many colleges without a foreign language, mathematics, or American or world history course. At Queens, however, we have instituted a sharply focused academic vision that engages College of Arts and Sciences students in a required interdisciplinary liberal arts program, an international experience involving 90 percent of our students, and a requirement that all students participate in a year-long internship related to their major. Several other schools are adopting a similar focus.

Two negative consequences have ensued from America's public policy on higher education:

- By not incorporating the country's 1,500 private institutions as equal partners into public policy to handle explosive growth, the United States has weakened a historic treasure (our first colleges were private) that could have saved millions of dollars and provided much-needed richness to American higher education.
- By failing to utilize fully the private sector, undergraduate education has been impoverished. Too many undergraduates are in large classes taught by graduate students—bright but inexperienced teachers. It is sadly ironic that when we have millions of young people searching for meaning, we have failed to use the very institutions whose strength is nurturing, a quality especially among church-related institutions.

We ought to understand education as "an encounter with an intellectual tradition."

We ought to insist that colleges state precisely their missions.

We ought to involve private institutions as full partners in planning for higher education's future.

For thirty-eight years, as a professor, coach, dean, vice president and president, I have gone to work every morning at an institution committed to helping students find creative relationships between faith and reason, between the life of the mind and that "Impenetrable Mystery" at the center of life.

It has been a wild, but rewarding ride in response to a high calling I invite others to join.

("WHAT IS A UNIVERSITY FOR? DOES ANYONE KNOW?" *Charlotte Observer*, MARCH 29, 1998.)

Be a Thermostat, Not a Thermometer

[For Billy Wireman, education's central purpose is to enable the young to contribute to the ongoing American enterprise which is to build an enlightened and just society, to benefit from the free exchange of ideas provided by a democracy, and to succeed in the environment of opportunity they help to create. His metaphor for this accomplishment is the thermostat, an agent of change.]

As we open Queens's 141st year, we join more than 3,500 colleges and universities in welcoming 15 million students to a new year. In the frenzy of opening activities, let's not forget our mission: engaging students in a learning experience that leads them to become productive, creative citizens in a global community. Being true to the academy's highest calling in this transformational process, I emphasize three points that sharply define who we are.

1. We achieve our mission primarily, but not exclusively, through the life of the mind. The academy is the only institution in society that sees learning as an end within itself. Granted, the church, corporations, the news media, and the arts all have learning programs, but their learning objectives are designed for quite narrow and

specific ends. To us, intellectual curiosity and the joy of learning are tonics for the soul centered in what Czech Present Vaclav Havel described as an "orientation of the spirit" committed to Jefferson's idea of the commonweal. In communicating this spirit to the students, William Wordsworth's wisdom comes to mind: "What we have loved others will love, and we will teach them how." Let's teach students to love intellectual curiosity and serious scholarship.

2. All issues at some point become moral and intellectual, requiring both ethical and critical analysis. We must not be corralled by the quick and the easy, the popular and the expedient. Truth and justice will win in the end. John Gardner established a useful method for our important function when he said the world needs "Critical Lovers"—those who love family, country, church, and city, but know that we can always do better.

3. Last, let's distinguish between a thermometer, which records the temperature, and a thermostat, which changes it. In a special way, learning communities are thermostats: change agents who imbue students with new ideas and new possibilities. We have free enterprise in business, why not free enterprise in ideas that challenge the status quo? The road to holiness in this life is through the world of action. Without action, there is no progress. T. S. Eliot said it well: "Between the idea and the action, falls the shadow." Too many shadows make for a dark place.

In a spirit of collegiality, I challenge us to be thermo-stats dedicated to transforming human knowledge into human understanding and wisdom, reshaped into human hopes and human dreams.

("Be a Thermostat," *Charlotte Observer*, August, 28, 1998.)

CREATORS AND CARRIERS OF TRADITION

[Vaclav Havel is one of Dr. Wireman's heroes, as is evident in his many citations from the president of the Czech Republic. In an August 2000 speech at Tunghai University in South Korea, Dr. Wireman analyzed the challenges facing church-related universities in the 21st century. After posing the challenge of uniting faith and reason, Athens and Jerusalem, in a world infected with violence and poverty, the complexities of international trade and the information age, he concluded with these remarks on the role of the university in these challenging times.]

Czech Republic President Vaclav Havel makes two important points about learning communities. First, academic inquiry is a very humbling experience. The more we learn the more we discover there is to learn. Thus, humility is the mark of the true scholar. Second, academic communities are not only reflections of the religious, cultural, and intellectual traditions that have created and nurtured them, they are also creators and carriers of those traditions. Inherent in these roles is the responsibility of critiquing the degree to which society is living up to its highest expectations. Therefore, learning communities must occasionally "stand outside the walls" of the city and evaluate the degree to which rhetoric is being translated into reality. Finding creative, mutually enriching relationships between faith and reason is surely a commanding moral imperative for the 21st century. Graduating a steady number of committed women and men who embody this combination in their life and work would be a blessing to any institution in any society.

("CHALLENGES FACING THE CHURCH-RELATED UNIVERSITY IN THE 21ST CENTURY," UNPUBLISHED SPEECH DELIVERED AT TUNGHAI UNIVERSITY, SOUTH KOREA, AUGUST, 2000.)

THE RELEVANCE OF LIBERAL EDUCATION

[During his lifetime in education, Billy Wireman was above all a person of action, a doer, a manager, a leader. He never attempted to construct a systematic philosophy of education. Yet there's no denying that certain themes recur throughout his thinking. What is education? Education is a process. What sort of process? It is a process of transformation, of change, of growth. Transformation of what? Of people's souls. It is a process of transformation by which people become more enlightened, wiser, more humane; it is a process that enables persons to flourish. To flourish? Yes, to flourish as practical persons who can do the world's work, and also as thinkers, poets, visionaries, who can imagine worlds yet to be. To flourish above all as free citizens in a free world, as citizens who are free and equal and able and willing to construct a better world. How is this all brought about? It's brought about especially by engaging students in the liberal arts, in a small, humane, personal setting, in which they are guided not by information technicians but by wise teachers. What do they learn? They learn how to connect wisdom with wisdom and thought with life; to connect the local with the global; to connect the worldly with the Transcendent. Above all, they learn service. And what powers all this? Zest. Energy. Excitement. A spirit at home in the midst of change and eager

for the next frontier. A spirit humble but also unafraid, realistically aware of human sin, but optimistically confident of God's grace. And at the center of all this is the student. Throughout his more than thirty years as a college president, nothing delighted Dr. Wireman more than being with students, in the classroom, in a coffee house, in the cafeteria. After an informal meeting with Queens students in 2000, Dr. Wireman jotted down some of his impressions which he later shared with the Queens faculty.]

It was one of those lively discussions that reminded me why I chose higher education: Over lunch with a group of Queens students this summer, the conversation turned to the relevance of liberal education in today's increasingly market-driven world. "It has never been more relevant," I contended. "And here's why: all human activity is conducted in a social, political, and economic milieu. Failure to understand the forces that create this milieu will lessen one's chances of living a rewarding, productive life of competence and caring."

"What do you mean by liberal education?" a student asked.

At the August 23, 2000, Queens opening faculty meeting, I answered that question:

A person is liberally educated when one can comprehend and transform the forces coming to bear on us all into a creative response characterized by finely honed skill and moral vigor. This requires four professional qualities:

1. UNDERSTANDING THE FORCES THAT HAVE SHAPED THE MODERN WORLD. In the West, we are products of Greek intellectual curiosity, Roman commitment to justice, the Judeo-Christian concern for "the least of these," and the moral courage and enterprise of leaders like Thomas Jefferson, Adam Smith, Mother Teresa, and Martin Luther King, among others. We must build on this combination of rationality, justice, stewardship, and enterprise. The civil rights, women's, and environmental movements have enriched these traditions by reminding us to be more inclusive.

2. COMPETENCE IN THE WORK PLACE. There was a time when preparation for work was low on the Academy's agenda. Now, finding connections between the classroom and the application of the insights and skills learned there to professional competence and fulfillment is critical to developing liberally educated citizens.

3. A FUNDAMENTAL GRASP OF A *BODY* OF KNOWLEDGE. This competence comes through the major. Importantly, while many students pursue professional opportunities in their major, numerous studies confirm that a liberal education facilitates one's professional advancement in any field.

4. AN UNDERSTANDING OF GLOBALIZATION. All of the above should be folded into an understanding that globalization is the one "BIG" development in the world

today. "A lively encounter" with a culture other their own helps students develop a deepening international curiosity.

Alexander Hamilton advanced the proposition that people will be ruled either by "reflection and choice" or "accident and force."

Reflection and choice require liberal education.

(Opening Statement to Queens College faculty, August 23, 2000.)

Epilogue

In June 2002, Billy O. Wireman retired as president of Queens College and was succeeded by Dr. Pamela Lewis. The Queens communications office prepared a fact sheet summarizing Dr. Wireman's career. Here are some of its highlights:

- He was America's youngest college president when he became president of Florida Presbyterian College in 1968, at age thirty-five.
- When he retired in 2002, he was the second-longest serving college president in America (just behind President Norman Wiggins of Campbell University).
- He was Queens College's longest-serving president.
- He had helped three of his vice presidents to become presidents of their own colleges and another vice president to become head of school at a college preparatory school.
- He had written or co-authored four books and more than 250 articles.
- He had served on innumerable church and civic organizations and had served for several years as chair of

both the Charlotte World Affairs Council and the Charlotte Community Relations Commission.

- He had received countless honors and awards from organizations around the world.
- Over his career, he raised some $175 million for education.
- In 60 international trips, he has lectured on every continent except Australia and Antarctica.
- What would Dr. Wireman miss most? "My interactions with the students and faculty and the intellectual stimulation of a college campus."
- What would he miss least? "The fact that for the last thirty-three years I have been responsible for raising $10,000 per day. No, I won't miss that!"
- What was his most special memory of Queens College? "When I walked into the President's Office, on Valentine's Day, 1978, my first day on the job, the desk was empty save for a vase with a single red rose in it. Attached to the vase was a note from Board of Trustees Chairman Bill Lee (also the Chairman of Duke Power Company). The note said: "Billy, we love you. May you long endure.""
- Now, on the occasion of his retirement, how does he view the future? To answer, he recited a phrase he learned in private pilot school: "CAVU—clear and visibility unlimited."

Acknowledgments

CREATING THIS BOOK was a labor of love, and there were many laborers in the field. We want to thank:

Joseph Grier, who has for many a year now taken time from his practice of the law to be a constant friend and benefactor to Queens College. This book was Mr. Grier's idea and it would never have come about without his enthusiastic leadership.

Tamara Leavell, Billy Wireman's tireless administrative assistant, who nudged this project along from inception to completion with great skill and unfailing cheer.

Our editors at NewSouth Books, especially Randall Williams and Suzanne La Rosa; they took our first ideas and very rough work and transformed them into a handsome book.

Billy Wireman. We know Dr. Wireman well enough to know that he prefers concision to effusion, but we want to thank him for giving us a completely free hand with his words and ideas, and even more, for giving us not only powerful leadership but rich friendship.

Finally, we want to thank those friends and colleagues who encouraged us along this book's long way.

D.G. & B.W.